ATTACK YOUR GIANTS

*Using King David's Perspective To Overcome any **Goliath** You Face*

ATTACK YOUR GIANTS

*Using King David's Perspective To Overcome any **Goliath** You Face*

Donnye D. Collins, Sr.

CSCM PUBLISHING, LLC
Maryland

Author neither implies directly nor indirectly nor otherwise purports to render medical, legal or clinical advice to those suffering from addictions or medical issues. It is advised that you seek professional counseling, medical or clinical assistance in order to address your particular situation. The advice suggested in this book is solely based on the author's interpretation of biblical meaning and accounts.

CSCM Publishing, LLC Books Subsidiary Rights Department, Germantown, MD 20874

Library of Congress Cataloging-in-Publication Data

Collins Sr. Donnye D
Attack Your Giants: Using King David's Perspective to Overcome any Goliath you Face / Donnye D Collins, Sr.

ISBN-13: 978-0-615-34502-4
ISBN-10: 0-615-35402-6

First Edition, 2009

CSCM PUBLISHING, LLC
Germantown, MD 20874

Edited by: Dr. Debra Chance
Cover Design: Tolu Onasanya: Conceptual Creations
Web/Graphic Designs

Dedication

I dedicate this book to my parents and grandparents from whom all love flows. You gave me the opportunity to live a life free of strife and heartache, and full of love, hope, and promise. You taught me to never quit, especially when someone's counting on you. Your sacrifices and direction permitted me to know what love and gratitude is. Although you are no longer on the earth, your spirit lives on in me, as I try to give back the love and compassion you instilled in me.

To my daughter, Tranise, my son, Donnye, Jr. grandson, Terryen, and granddaughter, Asia, thank you for the joy that you bring to my life. All of you are gifts from God.

Last, but certainly not least, to my loving wife, Christine, WOW, what a journey! You have been there for and with me from day one. I cannot put into words the depth and breadth of my love and admiration for you. You are the best life partner I could have ever dreamed up.

The Lord is my shepherd; I shall not want.

He makes me to lie down in green pastures; He leads me beside the still waters.

He restores my soul; He leads me in the paths of righteousness For His name's sake.

Yea, though I walk through the valley of the shadow of death, I will fear no evil; For You are with me; Your rod and Your staff, they comfort me.

You prepare a table before me in the presence of my enemies; You anoint my head with oil; My cup runs over.

Surely goodness and mercy shall follow me all the days of my life; And I will dwell in the house of the LORD Forever.

(Psalm 23: 1-6)

David

Table of Contents

Foreword

I count it a great honor and privilege to write this foreword on behalf of my son in the Lord, Donnye D. Collins, Sr. who has been a visionary member of our ministry for many years.

Attack Your Giants is a unique look at a familiar story that serves as a blueprint for anyone wanting to defeat the enemy once and for all. Donnye uses his many years of experience in the business world, his personal trials and triumphs and his acute knowledge of God's Word to convince us that we can confront our fears, get over our past, and use our God-given weapons to engage in battle.

In the arena of sports, I was always taught that the best offense is a strong defense. While this may be true for athletics, in the realm of spiritual warfare, the body of Christ has been on defense too long. It's time to go on the offensive in Jesus name!

The bible states in Ephesians 3:20 "Now unto Him that is able to do exceeding abundantly above all that we ask or think, according to the power that worketh in us." *Attack Your Giants* signifies that the same God that allowed David to defeat a lion, a bear and the great Philistine giant Goliath, is able by faith to give us the power to prevail over every giant in our lives also.

Giants manifest in our lives similar to the schoolyard bully we all faced growing up. Once we stood up to the bully, we found that the bully didn't have as much power as it appeared. In *Attack Your Giants,* Donnye, with the aid of the Holy Spirit, provides the strategies needed to conquer the strongholds that have tried to bully us most of our lives.

Experience has taught us if you don't attack your giants, **your giants will attack you.** This book is a must read for every child of the Kingdom who is ready to engage their Giant in battle and triumph over it!

Bishop Dane Andre' Coleman
Senior Pastor and Overseer
Greater New Hope Church and Ministries

Acknowledgements

I thank Almighty God, my Creator! There are no words that can be formulated by man that can do You justice. If I live one hundred years, I still couldn't describe the breadth and depth of the love I have for you! You have shown a grace and mercy towards me and mankind that defies comprehension. You are "The Creator of all things good and joyous!" Thank you for choosing me for this project.

I thank my Lord and Savior Jesus Christ from whom all blessings flow. You are my true Lord and Savior, my King of kings, my Prince of the peace I enjoy, and the Rock of my salvation. You are my EVERYTHING. You've been with me through this entire process. Your love and presence have kept me going even when I couldn't see or understand how things would turn out.

I thank the Holy Ghost. Your guidance, encouragement, insight and power have helped me through the toughest of times. Through your dedication and direction I have been able to come this far.

I thank my wife Christine for your unconditional love and support through this and all my many projects and endeavors and for hanging in there with me through all of the challenges we've experienced. I can't think of anyone else God could have yoked me with who would have brought me as much joy and happiness as you have. Thanks for being my wife and soul mate.

I thank my editor Dr. Debra Chance for your guidance and tireless efforts towards seeing this project come to fruition, and to my graphic artist Tolu Onasanya.

I thank all you who are blessed by this book. I pray it touches your life and spirit and is received with as much love and care in which it was conceived and written. I pray this book gives you a different perspective on conquering your Giants, and that you develop the courage to attack them, and achieve all that you are capable of so you can live your life with the fullness and richness God intended for you upon your creation.

Introduction

In this climate of world economic turmoil, job layoffs, government bailouts, record foreclosures, unbridled corporate greed and mismanagement; it seems as if we are in a vicious cycle of despair and hopelessness. With the twenty-four-hour news cycles constantly reporting only grim news of our economy, government, family and lifestyles changes, it seems as if circumstances are beyond our control, and just getting a reprieve from it all would be a welcomed release. The things or people we have come to rely on for relief and help in the past just aren't working anymore and no one seems to have any answers. Marriages and families are strained under the weight of financial uncertainty and economic tension. Mental, emotional, and financial challenges are clouding our minds and judgment causing the severance of longstanding personal and business relationships. It's no wonder more and more people feel as if they are being overcome by "Giants" and are trying to find some sense of meaning and direction in their lives.

In all of my years of observing people in personal, business, government, and spiritual settings, as well as being an avid student of God's word (the Bible), there is one thing I can truthfully say with a certainty, and that is, *"There is nothing new under the sun!"* Nothing! Everything we face as human beings has been faced or done by someone else at some point in the history of mankind. Every challenge we face today that looks like a Giant has been faced by someone before, especially when it comes to people in the Bible. One person who faced Giants and succeeded was David, the king of Israel. In those days, the greatest challenge that David and the nation of Israel faced were the Philistines. They intimidated and wreaked havoc upon them and were constantly warring against them for control of the land which God had promised Israel through their patriarch Abraham. Among the fighting men of the Philistine army was a giant by the name of Goliath. He instilled fear in men throughout the land. Standing over nine feet tall, he was a looming and intimidating presence. Dressed in his battle armor from head to toe, wielding his huge sword about and being boisterous with his loud and thunderous voice, the nation of Israel dreaded going into battle against him.

As a kid growing up in the church and even into my adult years, whenever I heard the story of David and Goliath, it was usually told as if Goliath attacked David and David successfully defended himself from the giant's onslaught by slaying him, but in reality that's not how the story went at all. The truth is it was the other way around. David ATTACKED Goliath! Read it for yourself! David went after Goliath. Why, you might ask? To David, Goliath stood in the way of everything that he held near and dear to his heart which was his God and his nation. Goliath threatened to jeopardize all that David loved and cared about. So in order for him to succeed in achieving his desire to bring honor to his God and his nation, David ATTACKED Goliath!

David was just a shepherd boy when his encounter with Goliath took place. One day while taking food to his brothers, who were fighting on the front lines of the battle between King Saul, who at the time was the king of Israel's army, and the Philistines, David overheard Goliath boastfully dishonoring God and the people of Israel. He was appalled that this giant would defy the armies of the Lord and instill fear in his people the way he did, so David decided to fight with the giant and kill him, therefore relieving them of the dreadful fear Goliath's presence created in them. David attacked and killed Goliath and restored the hope of his people in their God and in themselves. David later reigned as king of Israel and was considered by many to be the greatest king Israel ever had. There are monuments that were erected by him and in his name that still stand in Israel today. There's even a city in Israel named in his honor called the "City of David." This, as well as many of the teachings and doctrines he instituted during his reign, are still prevalent in Israel today as a testament to how much he was revered:

And he said: "Blessed be the Lord God of Israel, who has fulfilled with His hands what He spoke with His mouth to my father David, saying: 'Since the day that I brought My people out of the land of Egypt, I have chosen no city from the tribe of Israel in which to build a house, That My name might be there, nor did I choose any man to be a ruler over My people Israel. Yet I have chosen Jerusalem, that My name may be there, and I have chosen David to be over My people Israel.'
(2 Chronicles 6: 4-6)

David was so significant to God, that He chose Jesus Christ to be born of the same linage; as a direct descendant of David:

"I, Jesus, have sent My angel to testify to you these things in the churches. I am the Root and the Offspring of David."
(Revelation 22: 16)

Incredible! David's contribution to the nation of Israel is unmatched, both then and now. David was considered a "Man after God's own Heart." Yet, with all that David accomplished in his life, he was still a man with Giants.

I think most people can identify with David and his story because, not only did he have the physical giant Goliath to contend with, but he was a man who had other Giants in his life to deal with as well, the likes of which we've all experienced as human beings; financial setback, marriage failure, unruly children, unethical bosses, uncontrolled passions, yet he was able to accomplish all that he did primarily because of his personal and loving relationship with the Lord his God, a relationship you can develop with God also.

Although he is known for defeating the giant Goliath, David also wrote most of the book of Psalms. The book of Psalms gives you a perfect illustration of the love, reverence, dependence and honor David had for God, and how he sought God's leadership, direction and protection in nearly every area of his life. It also gives you an intimate look at the frank and honest conversations David had with God. I suggest you read it for more Giant fighting scriptures and affirmations.

David applied certain knowledge and principles to defeat and kill Goliath. He wasn't the king of Israel at the time he attacked Goliath, nor was he the prince next in line to the throne of the kingdom, but he was CHOSEN by Almighty God for a purpose, and so are you! Yes, YOU! Don't let anyone tell you otherwise. God chose YOU for His plan and purpose and He will give you whatever you need to accomplish it, including the ability to attack and conquer the Giants you face, like he did with David. However, you need to learn as David did how to access God's power to overcome any obstacle you face and understand His plan for your life.

"Giants" is simply a metaphor for the fear of a person, fear of rejection, a circumstance or situation (real and imagined), habit or addiction, vice, debt, market uncertainty, loss of home, job, money, or maybe a medical condition or weight problem, or anything that is stopping you cold in your tracks, intimidating you, creating a sense of despair, helplessness and loss of confidence and security in your life. Now is the time to deal with them for good. Are you ready to conquer and defeat these Giants forever? If so, do what David did, ATTACK THEM! That's right! Attack them, go after them! I know they seem to have the upper hand on you right now, but I am here to declare that the victory is yours! I want to show you how you can conquer these Giants that have plagued and hindered your progress and seek the life that God has promised you.

Perhaps it seems like you are in a situation similar to David where all that you hold near and dear to your heart- your peace of mind, family, security, finances, mortgage, credit and good name seem to be threatened and under attack by Giants. You've tried to defend yourself against the adverse effects that these Giants are having on you, but unlike David, you seem to be having little or no success against them. It should give you great assurance and hope to know that the same God that loved, guided, protected and directed David through his attack will do the same for you.

If there are Giants standing in the way of what you hold near and dear to your heart that is keeping you from the life you have imagined and dreamed of for yourself, your family or business, *Attack Your Giants* will show you how to apply and exercise your rights as a chosen one of God to conquer, defeat and overcome them. Now is the time to go after your Giants. You have the power to eliminate these Giants from your life once and for all! You don't have to be stressed, oppressed and defeated any longer. The victory can be yours.

Goliath just happened to be in the wrong place at the wrong time facing the wrong ONE! **David wasn't the victim, the GIANT was! Your Giants will be also!**

ATTACK YOUR GIANTS!
Donnye D. Collins, Sr.

Chapter One

David, an Unlikely Candidate...Oh Really?

The Lord has sought for Himself a man after His own heart, and the Lord has commanded him to be commander over His people,

(1 Samuel 13: 14)

> *"Every person must decide whether to walk in the light of creative altruism or in the darkness of destructive selfishness. This is the judgment. Life's most persistent and urgent question is, what are you doing for others?"*
>
> Martin Luther King, Jr.

The Cost of Disobedience

When Samuel, the priest and a prophet of God, made the above statement to Saul, the first and current king of Israel, it was after Saul had disobeyed God's law of only allowing a "*high priest*" to present ceremonial burnt offerings and sacrifices to Him before crucial events or an as atonement for sins:

> Then the Lord spoke to Moses, saying, "This is the law of the burnt offering: The burnt offering shall be on the hearth upon the altar all night until morning, and the priest shall put on his linen garment, and his linen trousers he shall put on his body."
> (Leviticus 6: 8-10)

God had given Moses and the children of Israel specific laws and instructions about how various offerings were to be made to Him, who was to make them, and for what purpose. Saul was a king, not a priest, who acted hastily out of fear of the Philistines and therefore did not follow God's instructions, but fear is never a reason or an excuse to disobey God. We often do the same thing when we allow fear to dictate our actions and those actions disobey God's direct and explicit instructions. Fear Giants are costly and destructive when we allow them to override God's law.

Saul was preparing to go into battle with the Philistine army with three thousand chosen fighting men from Israel. Two thousand of them were with him in Michmash, to the north, in the country of Bethel, and one thousand of the men were with Jonathan, his son, in Gibeah, to the south, in the city of Benjamin. Jonathan then launched an attack against the Philistine army at a garrison outpost in Geba and was successful in defeating them. When the Philistines heard about the attack, they assembled thirty thousand chariots and six thousand horsemen and went to Michmash to fight against Israel. Then Saul went to Gilgal as he was instructed by Samuel to do, and he summoned his men to Gilgal to join him:

> *"You shall go down ahead of me to Gilgal; and I will surely come down to you to offer burnt offerings and make sacrifices of peace offerings. Seven days you shall wait, till I come to you and show you what you should do."*
>
> *(1 Samuel 10: 8)*

When the men of Israel saw that the Philistine army greatly outnumbered theirs and had begun to advance towards them to do battle, they and the people of Israel became distressed and fled and hid in caves, thickets, rocks and holes. Saul was in Gilgal waiting for Samuel to come and make a peace offering. When he saw that the people were afraid and were fleeing because of the advancing Philistine army, he took it upon himself to make the burnt offerings of peace and fellowship to God instead.

Now it just so happened that as soon as Saul had finished presenting the burnt offerings, Samuel showed up. When he saw what had taken place, Samuel said to Saul, "What have you done?"

Saul replied, "When I saw that the people were scattered from me and afraid and you did not come within the days appointed, and the Philistines were assembling to fight us and I had not made supplication to the Lord, I therefore felt compelled, and made the offering to the Lord myself." Samuel then said to Saul:

> *"You have done foolishly. You have not kept the commandment of the Lord your God, which He had commanded you. For now the Lord would have established your kingdom over Israel forever. But now your kingdom shall not continue."*
>
> *(1 Samuel 13-14)*

These continuous acts of disobedience not only cost Saul the kingdom of Israel, but more importantly, they cost him God's favor and protection! He allowed his fears and impatience as well as his circumstances to circumvent God's laws and instructions. Your fears, impatience and disobedience can bring Giants into your lives that are costly emotionally, financially, and spiritually, as well. When you allow these Giants to make you take your eyes off God's law and promises and put them on your problems, no amount of reasoning or good intentions will prevent you from suffering the consequences of your actions.

After this encounter, Samuel made '*the*' statement to Saul that revealed to him as well as to you and me, the intention and desire God has for anyone who chooses to follow Him no matter what! He said to him:

> *"The Lord has sought for Himself a man after His own heart, and the Lord has commanded him to be commander over His people, because you have not kept what the Lord commanded you."*
>
> *(1 Samuel 13:14)*

David had not come on the scene yet when Samuel made this statement to Saul. Even though God told Samuel to tell Saul He would take the kingdom from him, God didn't do it immediately. Saul still ruled for quite some time after that incident, yet he continued to disobey God through error, bad judgment, ignorance, insecurity and often at times just plain stupidity. Isn't it wonderful that God doesn't give us what we deserve immediately when we deserve it or disobey Him, but He gives us a second, third, fourth and even more chances to get it right?

God Chooses David

Finally, after God had had enough of Saul's disobedience, He rejected him as king of Israel and sought to replace him. Afterwards, He sent Samuel to seek the next king of Israel from among the house of Jesse in Bethlehem:

> Now the Lord said to Samuel, "How long will you mourn for Saul, seeing I have rejected him from reigning over Israel? Fill your horn with oil, and go; I am sending you to Jesse the Bethlehemite. For I have provided Myself a king among his sons."
>
> *(1 Samuel 16: 1)*

When God sent Samuel to Bethlehem, He had to give him certain instructions; otherwise Samuel would have assumed he knew what to look for in the next king of Israel.

When God chose Saul to be the first king of Israel, Saul's appearance stood out:

> And He had a choice and handsome son whose name was Saul. There was not a more handsome person than he among the children of Israel. From his shoulders upward he was taller than any of the people.
>
> *(1 Samuel 9: 2)*

Naturally, after choosing Saul, he would have assumed that stature and physical appearance was part of God's '*criteria*' for choosing a king, so he was looking for someone who would fit that description this time as well, don't you think? Wrong! When Jesse paraded his handsome and physically strong sons before him for the choosing, Samuel took one look at them and assumed God would surely choose one of them and replied:

> *"Surely the Lord's anointed is before Him!"*
>
> *(1 Samuel 16: 6)*

God quickly corrected Samuel!

> *"Do not look at his appearance or at his physical stature, because I have refused him. For the Lord does not see as a man sees; for man looks at the outward appearance, but the Lord looks at the heart."*
>
> *(1 Samuel 16: 7)*

Wow! Don't we do that? Don't we judge people by how they look, what they have, where they live, what they drive, where their degree is from, and make all sorts of judgments and assumptions based on outward appearances? Many times the same kinds of judgments and assumptions are being made about us as well, don't you agree? Isn't it wonderful to know that God doesn't look at those things, but He looks at the *heart?* After Jesse had seven of his sons come before Samuel and none of them was the one, Samuel asked him, "Are all the young men here?" Then Jesse told him that he had his youngest son who was keeping the sheep. Samuel requested that he be brought to him. When David showed up, he probably wasn't what Samuel expected:

> *So he sent and brought him in. Now he was ruddy, with bright eyes, and good looking.*
>
> *(1 Samuel 16: 12)*

"Ruddy" means having a reddish complexion. Maybe not what Samuel was expecting, but it didn't matter. God chose him:

> *And the Lord said, "Arise, anoint him; for this is the one!"*
>
> *(1 Samuel 16: 12)*

God chose David, a "*shepherd*" boy to be the next king of Israel, but the key to this text is Samuel's actions once God told him to anoint David as king. This is a lesson we can all learn from that will save us so much heartache, stress and confusion. Regardless of what Samuel may have thought of God's choice and I can't say whether he gave it any thought, but if he did, he was careful to be obedient, respectful, and faithful to God's choice, and to the instructions God gave him, and carried them out without question, hesitation or reservation. He immediately did as he was instructed to do!

> *Then Samuel took the horn of oil and anointed him in the midst of his brothers; and the Spirit of the Lord came upon David from that day forward.*
>
> *(1 Samuel 16: 13)*

Samuel was obedient, not judgmental. How often has God blessed someone that maybe you thought shouldn't have been blessed, or perhaps you've judged somebody in terms of their looks, lifestyle, upbringing, then once you got to know them or heard their true story found your judgments and assumptions to be totally wrong and off base? Many times you don't know who is in your midst, and what you are missing out on when you judge or make unfounded assumptions about others.

Why David?

To understand why God chose David, the "Shepherd" boy, you have to understand **what** David was...David was truly a "shepherd!" He was a shepherd by choice; he loved being with the sheep. He loved everything about the sheep; it was his nature to be with the sheep. Now you might ask what does that have to do with anything? It has EVERYTHING to do with EVERYTHING! David's HEART was with the sheep! In other words, David had a *"SHEPHERD'S HEART!"* Why is this significant? This is significant because God said, *"He sought for Himself a man after His own heart!"*

Because God loved the children of Israel so much, he couldn't just entrust them to anybody again. Saul failed at being king because he started to serve his own interests and not those of God or of the people, and the Lord regretted that He had even made Saul king over Israel:

> *And Samuel went no more to see Saul until the day of his death, nevertheless Samuel mourned for Saul, and the Lord regretted that He had made Saul king over Israel.*
>
> (1 Samuel: 15: 35)

The person God chose this time had to have a shepherd's heart by nature. When you understand the character of a shepherd, and their desire to care for, nurture and protect the sheep or those who are in their care, you begin to see why God chose David.

God felt that choosing a person who had the **heart** for the job would best serve His people. When Saul ruled as king to the children of Israel he turned out to be a "hireling" instead of a shepherd. There is a distinct difference between a hireling and a shepherd. They both tend sheep; however, the two are worlds apart in their attitude towards their duties and responsibilities. Jesus, more than anyone best explains the difference:

> *"I am the good shepherd. The good shepherd gives His life for the sheep. But the hireling, he who is not the shepherd, one who does not own the sheep, sees the wolf coming and leaves the sheep and flees; and the wolf catches the sheep and scatters them. The hireling flees because he is a hireling and does not care about the sheep. I am the good shepherd; I know My sheep, and am known by My own. As the Father knows Me, even so I know the Father; and **I lay down my life for the sheep.**"*
>
> (John 10: 11-15)

Wow! Big difference, wouldn't you agree? Anyone who wants to lead in God's kingdom must have or develop certain "HEART QUALIFICATIONS!" Saul didn't have them. The children of Israel didn't know him nor did they consider him to be a good king. They couldn't relate to him and neither could he to them. David could. David's soldiers loved him and would have given their lives for him, and some did. The children of Israel loved him too, because he gave of himself for their needs. He was even willing to give his life for Saul's as we find later in their relationship. He often sacrificed for him. Shepherds are tender, kind, sincere, loving and intimate caretakers who guide, correct, protect, and feed their sheep. God saw that in David.

A Hireling

1. Labors only for the money
2. Has no heart for the sheep
3. Flees when trouble arises
4. Unfaithful to his master
5. Feeds himself first
6. Neglects the sheep
7. Drives the sheep hard

A Shepherd

1. Labors out of love
2. Loves them with his heart
3. Protects them from danger
4. Faithfully serves his master
5. Feeds the sheep first
6. Tends to the sheep
7. Wisely and carefully leads them

As you can see, there are stark differences between the two. David naturally had what God was looking for Saul didn't. David, the unlikely candidate, not hardly! David was simply the BEST person for the job. How about you? Honestly, which of these two descriptions do you best identify with in your current role as head of your family, business or community? Have you been a shepherd or a hireling to those you are in charge of or responsible for? Perhaps part of the reason why you may be facing the Giants that you are is because of how you are handling God's sheep. Are you bringing blessings or curses into your life?

We clearly see why God chose David for the task of leading His people. David had the heart for it. Is your heart conditioned to go where God leads you, or for leadership? David was able to attack the Giants in his life because he had favor with God and God was with him always, even through David's trails and challenges, both as a human man and a divine chosen leader. God has done the same for you. Because of Jesus Christ, in the eyes of God, you are no different than David. Through Him, God has granted you the same rights and privileges; however, it does help to have a sincere heart for God and the desire to do what He has called upon you to do with a willing spirit. When God is looking for someone to accomplish His will, He chooses people with the necessary characteristics for the job, or He helps you to develop them. He doesn't want you to get weighed down or held up by Giants. Since He has called you forth for His purpose and will, believe that He is able to see you through until the task is accomplished. He will give you the support; encouragement and insight you need to battle any Giant and be victorious!

So let's get started! How do you **Attack Your Giants?** How do you develop and apply the strategies, insights, mindset and beliefs like David did which allowed him to conquer and defeat Goliath and the other Giants he faced. What specific things must you do to began conquering and defeating your Giants? First...

Chapter Two

Replace **FEAR** with FEAR

Therefore I remind you to stir up the gift of God which is in you through the laying on of my hands. For God did not give you the spirit of fear, but of power and of love and of a sound mind.

(2 Timothy 1: 6-7)

"Courage is not the absence of fear, but the triumph over it. J felt fear myself...but J hid it behind a mask of boldness."

Nelson Mandela

We've all heard it or have seen it written somewhere, the most widely used definition of FEAR, and it goes like this:

False

Evidence

Appearing

Real

False evidence **"Appearing"** to be real! Fear is just that most of the time... just an "illusion." Are your Giants real or imagined? Giants are usually what YOU make them! They have power because YOU give them power. Nothing has power over you except the power you give it. If you give the Giant power to rule you, it will for as long as you allow it to. David knew this all too well; unfortunately the men of Israel didn't.

Goliath was an intimidating figure no doubt; his mere presence was causing grief and strife to the nation of Israel:

> *And a champion went out from the camp of the Philistines, named Goliath, from Gath, whose height was six cubits and a span. He had a bronze helmet on his head, and he was armed with a coat of mail, and the weight of the coat was five thousand shekels of bronze. And he had bronze armor on his legs and a bronze javelin between his shoulders. Now the staff of his spear was like a weaver's beam, and his iron spearhead weighed six hundred shekels; and a shield-bearer went before him.*
> *(1 Samuel 17: 4-7)*

Wow! Intimidating to say the least! Goliath was REAL, not imagined. Goliath and the Philistines had gathered their armies together to do battle with Israel at Sochoh in the land of Judah. They had encamped between Sochoh and Azekah, a strategic stronghold near Ehpes Dammim, (a city in Judah) which later became known for its frequent battles between Israel and the Philistines. Why this place in particular? Just like the Giants in your life that are in your face all the time trying to intimidate and scare you, the Philistines chose this location because it allowed them to be in Saul and the men of Israel's face all the time! Saul's army was gathered on the other side of the mountain just across the valley, so the Philistines were in plain view of Saul and the men of Israel.

Goliath taunted Israel for forty days straight, going to the edge of the battle line, morning and evening:

> *Then he stood and cried out to the armies of Israel, and said to them, "Why have you come out to line up for battle? Am I not a Philistine, and you the servants of Saul? Choose a man for yourselves, and let him come down to me. If he is able to fight with me and kill me, then we will be your servants. But if I prevail against him and kill him, then you shall be our servants, and serve us." When Saul and all Israel heard these words of the Philistine, they were dismayed and greatly afraid. And the Philistine drew near and presented himself forty days, morning and evening.*
> *(1 Samuel 17: 8-9, 11, 16)*

Isn't that the way it is with the Giants in your life? The fears, people, situations and circumstances you face, positioning themselves in your life to intimidate and discourage you? They stand boldly in plain view between where you are and where you want to be, mocking and taunting you! That extra weight, those unruly children, the threat of foreclosure, eviction or unemployment notices...Giants! Giants! Giants! When Goliath taunted the men of Israel in this manner, they were so frightened and afraid of him that they forgot how to fight or that they could. Like the men of Israel, you've always had the ability to fight, but your Giant's boisterous presence and taunting paralyzes you, and you forget that you even know how. There was no doubt that Goliath was a real and formidable foe for any person, army or nation; however, there was something that they could do about it. Yet, herein lies the most damaging effect Goliath had on the fighting men of Israel or that any Giant can have on you.

Not only did Goliath render them helpless in their minds, but worst, he rendered them HOPELESS. Hopelessness can have a debilitating effect on your mind, emotions and self esteem, and it discourages your desire to act. If you think a situation is hopeless, you won't be motivated to do anything about it? If this is your outlook, you are in a danger zone. You can never get so afraid of anyone or anything where you think nothing can be done about it. Never let any Giant, regardless of how big or intimidating it may be, render you hopeless. No Giant should have that much power and control in your life! David had a much different outlook on the situation. He didn't deny that Goliath and the Philistines existed. That was obvious; however his focus was not on them. David's focus was on his God! Therefore David was not hopeless in the face of seemingly overwhelming odds; instead, he put the situation in the proper perspective!

David replaced the **F**alse **E**vidence **A**ppearing **R**eal with- Focused Energy And Resolve.

Focused

Energy

And

Resolve

Focused Energy and Resolve means to focus your energies and efforts on the things you can control and do something about. Wasting time and energy focusing on things you can't control or change is very frustrating, discouraging and emotionally consuming. When you focus your energies on what can be done about a circumstance, situation or event, regardless of how small the steps might be in the beginning, you begin to retake control of your life and reshape your outlook and mindset. The "false fear" of what might happen is replaced by the "actual reality" of what *is* happening, because you are consciously focused on doing what is within your power to bring about the results you want and can control. Early in my business career I was fortunate to be mentored by a person whom I consider to be one of the greatest leaders in business and personal leadership. His name is Art Williams. He was the founder of A. L. Williams, a life insurance and securities company that in its day dominated the industry and set sales records that have yet to be broken in the industry. The following is one of Art's (as we would call him) greatest quotes that has helped me reset my focus when I find myself allowing fear and worry to cloud my judgment and thinking. It goes like this:

"99% of the things you worry about NEVER happen, so why worry!"

Isn't that true most of the time? Ninety nine percent of the things we worry about or fear happening never happen! How often have you found yourself worrying about or fearing something that could have happened but didn't? That was 'false evidence appearing real,' wouldn't you agree? Yet the time and energy you spent worrying and fearing what could happen was real; real time, real energy, real distraction! Can you get any of that time or energy back? Did anything change as a result of the worry and fear, time and effort you diligently put into it? Chances are NO, NOTHING CHANGED! On the other hand, what if the 1% that could have happened happens; what can you do about it? Probably a lot, because you would have been better prepared to deal with it, wouldn't you? You would be better prepared mentally, physically and emotionally to address it more effectively. As you focus your energy, time and attention on what's within your "sphere of control," you therefore influence the outcome of every situation you face. How confident would you be if you knew you could influence the outcome of your attack against your Giants?

The Resolve

Once you've decide to attack your Giants and eliminate the fear and control they've had in your life, you must also develop the resolve to stand by that decision no matter what happens. It's been said and proven that; "There is nothing more powerful on Earth than a made up mind!" When you have resolved in your mind to see your decisions through no matter what, there's also a calming peace that comes over you that is indescribable. It's a *peace in the midst of the storm.* When you've made a resolution to accept the consequences and challenges of your decisions, you become free, and your focus becomes clearer... if people decide to leave you, let them leave, if you lose the house, the car, the job, then so be it. From that moment on nothing and no one can stand in your way. Your Giants lose their power and stronghold over you. The key to making this kind of resolution is to decide once and for all that this is where you are going to make your stand and fight for what you want and believe in. With this kind of resolve and God's help and grace; nothing will stop you from having it.

I am sure when David was living in his father's house tending to his sheep that, fighting Philistines and Giants was the furthest thing from his mind. He was aware that the war was going on because his three eldest brothers went to fight with Saul and the men of Israel, but up to that point he had no intention of fighting anything except the wolves off of the sheep. Yet, like most of the Giants in your life, you weren't looking for them, but somehow they found you, wouldn't you agree?

One day David's father Jesse, told him to take food and rations to his brothers on the front lines and to check on them. He also sent some for the other troops. So David rose early in the morning to go and do what his father requested. He left the sheep in the care of a caretaker, his shepherd instinct, and set out on his journey to the battle lines. When he arrived at the valley where the fighting was taking place, he gave the rations for the troops to the supply keeper, and then he went down to the front line to deliver the food to his brothers. As he approached them, he heard and saw Goliath going to and fro, ranting and raving, speaking in the same boisterous and intimidating manner that he had become accustomed to doing. David saw how Goliath's presence and manner made the men of Israel become dreadfully afraid and flee from him.

This wasn't false evidence appearing real to David; Goliath existed, that was evident, but the men of Israel thought that he couldn't be defeated! In David's mind *that was false*. At that point, David resolved in his mind to fight Goliath and free his people from the mental bondage they were in. He knew that the Giant could be defeated. David didn't let anything about Goliath scare or intimidate him. Neither Goliath's stature, boisterous booming voice, nor the flailing around of his huge sword that had killed so many men scared David. Although David decided to put his energies into fighting Goliath, he put defeating him in God's hands. How about you? What scares you most about confronting your Giants? Whatever it is, you must deal with it now in order to move on and have the victory! What will it take for you to begin to focus your energies and efforts towards what you want to achieve and develop the resolution and commitment to defeat the Giants that stand in the way of you getting it? One of the most important factors I think you need to have that will help you develop the resolution necessary to defeat anything that stands in the way of you achieving your heart's desire and God's purpose for your life is to have a consuming WHY!

Check Your Motive

Who or what are you fighting for? This more than anything else will determine your success in conquering your Giants and achieving your desired outcome. If you are looking for God's divine help and protection to see you through to victory, then I suggest you check your motives. As David approached the troops, one of the men of Israel said to David, "Have you seen this man how he comes to defy Israel? Of any man who kills him, the king will enrich with great riches, and will give him his daughter to marry, and he and his father's house will be exempt from paying taxes." Now you really have to get this. Here this man is in a battle for his nation's very survival, facing a formidable foe, and maybe about to lose his own life and all he can think about is PERSONAL gain... 'MONEY AND WOMEN!' His priorities were totally mixed up.

What is your motive? What are your priorities? Why are you in the fight? Who will get the credit for your victory? Could it be that your Giant is your own selfishness? Are your priorities in sync with God's will for your life? Are you only looking at how something or someone affects you and your self centered desires? God wants to be the center of your life. In fact, the very first commandment He gave to the children of Israel at Mt. Sinai after they left the bondage of Pharaoh in Egypt was to keep their priorities and focus straight:

"I am the Lord your God, who brought you out of the land of Egypt, out the house of bondage. You shall have no other gods before Me. You shall not make for yourself a carved image— any likeness of anything that is in heaven above, or that is in

*the earth beneath, or that is in the water under the earth; you
shall not bow down to them nor serve them. For I, the Lord
your God, am a jealous God"*

(Exodus: 20: 1-4)

God knows it is in man's nature to get sidetracked and in turn
begin to develop selfish motives and desires. This is the thinking of
many people who are battling Giants and having little or no success.
Their priorities and focus are on the wrong things. Your chances of a
breakthrough are slim, and your Giant will defeat you every time.
The reason David was able to accomplish all that he did and
continued to have the love and confidence of God, can be found in
the next statement David made to the soldier. This displays the
essence of David's character:

*Then David spoke to the men who stood by him, saying, "What
shall be done for the man who kills this Philistine and takes
away the reproach from Israel? For who is this uncircumcised
Philistine, that he should defy the armies of the living God?"*

(1 Samuel 17: 26)

David's first concern was not for himself, but for the peace and
welfare of his people. He saw firsthand how they cowered in fear of
Goliath and seemed helpless and hopeless at his mere presence. He
was disturbed by how this giant affected their behavior toward God
and each other. David also saw how they had taken their eyes off of
God's divine protection for them and focused more on the Philistine
army. He felt that by removing these threats from the psyche of his
people, they would be free to serve God without worry. They would
know that God fought for them and would deliver them from the
hand of Goliath and the Philistines. David even went as far as to
question the intelligence of Goliath, as if to say, 'You've got some
nerve even going up against the people of the LIVING GOD anyway!
Does he know who he's fooling with?' David's attitude was... 'If you
don't know, you'd better ask somebody!' David knew that his God was
much bigger than any Giant, Goliath or otherwise, but his motive for
fighting had to be much bigger than himself!

Check your Perspective

How BIG is God in your fight? That's right, HOW BIG IS GOD IN YOUR FIGHT? Perhaps the reason you have not been able to gain any ground or conquer the Giants you've faced in the past is due to your perception of God in relation to your Giant. Is the perception of your Giant equally matched to the perception of your GOD? You might be asking....what does he mean by being 'equally matched?' What I mean is, perhaps *your perception of God is really no bigger than the size of your Giant.* You may be trying to fight your 'house or car payment that's overdue' Giant with a house or car payment SIZE image of God, your 'foreclosure or eviction' Giant with a foreclosure or eviction SIZE image of God, a 'medical and drug addiction' Giant with a medical and drug addiction SIZE image of God, a 'weight loss' Giant with a weight loss SIZE image of God, etc! Like I said earlier, regardless of who or what your Giant represents, *if your image of God is no bigger than your problem, you will continue to fight a losing battle.* You are SEEING God as being the same size as you are SEEING your problem. They are 'EQUALLY MATCHED' in size and scope. Again, I ask you; "How BIG is your image of God in relation to your Giant?" Get this fact in your spirit. A principle that David learned and applied, and that is:

You will only get from God what you can believe Him for! NO MORE, no LESS!

If you believe God is only as big as your house or car payment, then that's about all you will get....a house or car payment. If you believe God is only big enough to give you enough to get by, then that's all you will get....enough to get by, and all you have is a "get by god." *So many times your perception of God is no bigger than the problems you want Him to solve for you.* You certainly aren't seeing Him as being big enough to help you attack and defeat the Giants in your life. You've got to change your thinking and perception of who God is! You are thinking too small. You've boxed our Mighty,

Awesome, Limitless God into your small thinking and perception. He is so much greater than you're seeing Him to be. If you want to win in the fight, start seeing **Him** for who **He** is:

As your **CREATOR:** *In the beginning God created the heavens and the earth.*

(Genesis 1: 1)

As your **SUSTAINER:** *Forty years You sustained them (the children of Israel) in the wilderness; They lacked nothing; Their clothes did not wear out and their feet did not swell.*

(Nehemiah 9: 21)

As your **PROVIDER:** *But my God shall supply ALL your needs according to His riches in glory By Christ Jesus.*

(Philippians 4: 19)

As your **PROTECTOR:** *My defense is of God, Who saves the upright in heart.*

(Psalm 7: 10)

Reset your focus! Focus on the SIZE of God, not the size of the Giant. Only by checking your motive for why you are fighting to begin with and resetting your view and perception of how big and omnipotent God is will you be able to BOLDY attack and conquer your Giants! You will also gain a better understanding of why you haven't been successful in the past. This applies to any Giant you face and is crucial to your success in the battle. Fear didn't grip David because he was clear on WHO his God was, and had confidence that God was much BIGGER than anything he faced. He couldn't understand how anyone didn't see God the way he saw God! The men of Israel were fighting with an attitude that the fight was theirs. They only saw the Giant because that's what they focused their energies on... 'the Giant.' They're trust was in their abilities to fight the Giant themselves. Often, when you only see the Giant, it's because that's all you're focused on 'THE GIANT' and on your own abilities to fight it with your limited mind, resources and energies! Keep your priorities straight. Keep "the main thing the main thing."

David focused his energies on what he and HIS GOD could do, not the giant! He resolved in his mind that he had nothing to fear. Increase the size of God's presence and abilities in your life. God is ready, willing and more than able to conquer any Giant you face. He did not give you the spirit of fear; you developed that on your own. He gave you the POWER to conquer what you can, HIS GRACE to accept what you can't, and a SOUND MIND to know the difference!

> *There shall no man be able to stand before you: for the Lord your God shall lay the FEAR of you and the dread of you upon all the land that ye shall tread upon, as He hath said to you.*
> *(Deuteronomy 11:25 KJV)*

Replace the **FEAR** that immobilizes you with the FEAR that empowers you, the **FEAR** of what you can't control with the FEAR of what you can!

Chapter Three

Release Your PAST!

Not that I have already attained, or am already perfected; but I press on, that I may lay hold of that for which Christ Jesus has also laid hold of me. But one thing I do, forgetting those things which are behind and reaching forward to those things which are ahead, I press towards the goal of the prize of the upward call of God in Christ Jesus.

(Philippians 3: 13)

"I'm convinced more than ever that man finds himself liberation only when he binds himself to God and commits himself to his fellow man."

Ronald Reagan

Y our "PAST" is defined as:

Psychological

Acts

Suspending Your

Todays

Wouldn't you agree that the toughest Giants you battle are the ones that are psychological, and are usually brought on by something that happened to you *in* the past? These Giants threaten to keep you in bondage indefinitely until they are dealt with and defeated. Psychological Giants threaten the joy, happiness, peace and purpose you could be experiencing today. You must attack them and minimize or eliminate the stronghold they have on you. These Giants are the acts of fear, injustice, domination, insensitivity or selfishness that were perpetrated on you by someone, or that you brought upon yourself. They are suspending your enjoyment of today and threaten your tomorrow. They are psychological because they affect your mind, your thinking. Past hurts, failures, relationships, sins, even successes, have a way of keeping you from reaching for something greater by making you think you don't deserve it, or that you can't achieve it based on what someone said or did to you '*in the past.*' The constant reflection of what happened and the replaying of it over and over in your mind is limiting your actions and your enjoyment of today.

They are also psychological because they serve as the mental ties that still have you bound to that act or event as if it occurred recently. The actual event may have happened some time ago, but the emotional and psychological scars associated with it are just as real today as they were then. The guilt, fear, shame, anger, and dread associated with these acts still seem to have a hold on you even though they may have occurred earlier in your life, perhaps even as early as your childhood. Whether real or imagined, they are just as paralyzing today as they were when they first occurred. You may be going through the motions of living, but you still can't seem to shake the stronghold they have on you.

David's PAST could have affected his ability to function and be victorious over Goliath, as well as limit his ability to defeat the other Giants he encountered later in his life, but he didn't allow it to. Instead he chose to focus on God and His ability to deliver him from any enemy, seen or unseen. David had challenges early in his life too. He was the youngest of eight sons of his father Jesse. He was mistreated by his older brothers and was often left alone with the sheep. When his father sent him to take the food to his brothers and check on them, he encountered a grilling from his older brother Eliab:

When Eliab, David's older brother, heard him speaking with the men, he burned with anger at him and asked, "Why have you come down here? And with whom did you leave those few sheep in the desert? I know how conceited you are and how wicked your heart is; you came down only to watch the battle." "Now what have I done?" said David. "Can't I even speak?"

(1 Samuel 17: 28-29 NIV)

I am sure this was not the first encounter like this between David and his brothers, and even though he was just a boy, he didn't let the verbal abuse affect him. Early in David's life, some of his greatest psychological challenges came at the hand of Saul. Before David's encounter with Goliath, he was summoned to the palace to become Saul's armor bearer and harpist. Because of Saul's jealousies, insecurities, and anger after David's victory over Goliath, he was under constant persecution, threat and duress at the hand of the Saul. Even though God had stripped the kingdom from Saul and had appointed Samuel to anoint David to be the next king of Israel (Saul was unaware of it at the time), David still served him faithfully, even under these trying circumstances.

When the distressing spirits came upon Saul, David, being a musician, often played the harp to soothe him. But Saul's constant paranoia soon made him become afraid of David until one day while David was playing the harp, Saul threw a spear at him and tried to pin him to the wall. From that day forward Saul relentlessly sought to kill David. Can you imagine having to live and work under those kinds of conditions-your boss plotting to kill you, or at least kill your career every day? Later, after David's victory over Goliath, as promised, Saul gave his daughter Michal to David to wed, just to have her try to entrap him. I am sure having your boss who is also your father-in-law enlist the aid of his daughter, your wife, to plot to have you killed would have a tremendous psychological effect on you! Talk about stress! Now that's an emotional PAST Giant, yet David held up under the pressure and constant threats in his life.

Throughout their relationship, which spans some twenty years, Saul was constantly trying to kill David or sought to have someone else do it. David was often on the run from him, however, there arose two separate occasions when David had the opportunity to kill Saul, yet he chose not to because he felt it was not his place to kill the person God had originally chosen to be king of Israel. Besides, David really loved and respected Saul as God's chosen man. Even though David knew that God had taken the kingdom from Saul, he felt if God put him there, then it would be God who removed him. David was loyal to Saul no matter what. He served him with integrity and honor. By doing so, David prevailed. He kept his mind free of anger and bitterness towards Saul.

How about you? Has someone in your past caused tremendous heartache, loss of family, money, peace of mind, fear or disruption in your life like Saul did to David? Are you holding on to the Giant of resentment, hurt, pain that you suffered because of someone else's actions towards you? You might be justifying your anger towards them for what they did to you, but to what avail? As long as you hold on to the pain, bitterness, and resentment of what happened, that person or situation still has power over you.

David had the opportunity to kill Saul on two separate occasions, and he could have done so without being discovered. Once, when David and his trusted fighters were hiding in the back of a cave in the wilderness of Ziph, unaware that David and his men were there, Saul entered the cave to relieve himself. David's men thought this was a sign that God had delivered Saul into David's hands so David could kill him, but David refused to do so. However, he did cut off a corner of Saul's robe to show him later just how close he was to him without him knowing it. Afterwards, even that small act of cutting Saul's robe troubled David:

> And he said to his men, "The Lord forbid that I should do this thing to my master, the Lord's anointed, to stretch out my hand against him, seeing he is the anointed of the Lord."
>
> *(1 Samuel 24: 6)*

David not only chose not to harm Saul, but he kept his men from harming Saul also. After Saul left the cave, David soon followed him undetected. When Saul got a far distance from the cave, David called out to him and told him what had happened, about how he cut a corner of his robe and could have killed him if he wanted to, "But my eye spared you," he said, "Let the Lord judge between you and me, and let the Lord avenge me on you, but my hand shall not be against you."

If given the opportunity to exact vengeance upon someone who has wronged you and caused you so much grief and anguish, and you could do it without them or anyone knowing about it, what would you do? Honestly!

On another occasion David and his most trusted fighter Abishai came upon Saul sleeping in an outpost city after Saul had chased David with three thousand chosen men of Israel. To avoid being discovered, David and Abishai stayed in the wilderness just outside of the city. When they came upon Saul sleeping, Abishai asked David if he could kill him right there:

> *So David and Abishai came to the people by night; and Saul lay sleeping within the camp, with his spear stuck in the ground by his head. Then Abishai said to David, "God has delivered your enemy into your hands this day. Now therefore, please let me strike him at once with the spear, right to the earth; and I will not have to strike him a second time!" But David said to Abishai, "Do not destroy him; for who can stretch out his hand against the Lord's anointed, and be guiltless?" David said furthermore, 'As the Lord lives, the Lord shall strike him, or his day shall come to die, or he shall go out to battle and perish. The Lord forbid that I should stretch out my hand against the Lord's anointed.'*
>
> *(1 Samuel 26: 7-11)*

David understood and honored what God said to Moses about vengeance:

"Vengeance is Mine, and recompense; Their foot shall slip in due time; For the day of their calamity is at hand, And the things to come hasten upon them."

(Deuteronomy 32: 35)

David's attitude and mindset was that **God is the One who executes revenge.** He didn't have to worry or be stressed about getting even with or getting back at Saul for what he had done to him. David knew that nothing Saul did to him would escape God's attention or justice, and it wasn't up to him to determine Saul's fate. He felt God would execute justice upon Saul as He saw fit. All David could do was forgive him, and move on with living the life God has for him.

Can you forgive your Giants, regardless of how much pain they have inflicted upon you? How often do you find yourself angered or stressed over something someone has done to you? How long have you harbored those ill feelings toward that person or that situation? Where has it gotten you up to now? Do what David did. Release your PAST or the people now! Let God deal with them as He sees fit. Nothing that has happened to you has escaped God's attention or justice. In order to fulfill your desire to lead a happy, productive, joyous life, you must release your PAST! Don't let these psychological acts suspend your enjoyment of today! Reset your focus on where God is taking you, and all that He has in store for you. Understand that what happened to you DOES NOT represent WHO you are. David was a king, PERIOD! Nothing that he experienced with Saul changed the fact that HE WAS A KING chosen by ALMIGHTY GOD to lead the nation of Israel through its greatest revolution and later its reunification! What if David had allowed those psychological acts of Saul's or his brothers to keep him from his destiny? The nation of Israel would have suffered greatly.

You have been chosen by the same God who chose David to perhaps lead your family, a business, civic or charitable organization, political post, PTA, school, classroom, whatever it may be. You have to free yourself from the PAST Giants which threaten to hinder you and keep you from maximizing your fullest potential and all you know you can give to reach your destiny!

PAST Giants to Conquer

PAST Giants manifest in your life in different forms. Regardless of what form they take, the results are the same. You are held up from living a life full of joy, peace, love and happiness.

Here are the most common PAST Giants you fight everyday:

Your EMOTIONAL PAST

Your PHYSICAL PAST

Your FINANCIAL PAST

Your MENTAL PAST

Let's look at how each of these Giants of your PAST disrupts your lives and how you can defeat them.

EMOTIONAL PAST- Rape, incest, molestation, divorce, heartbreak

Usually this one is at the hands of something someone did to you. It tends to have the greatest stronghold on you and hinders you from enjoying your life to the fullest today. You may feel like the pain, hurt and humiliation you suffered at the hands of someone else was just too much to bear. To be put in a situation where you felt helpless and unprotected was just too much to endure for you to forgive and forget. Maybe you are right; however, what I am suggesting is that you look at it from a different perspective.

RESET YOUR FOCUS! While you can't always do much about what happened to you, you can always do something about how long YOU allow it to affect you, don't you agree? Consider what Jesus said on the matter:

"Do not fear those who kill the body but cannot kill the soul.
But rather fear Him who is able to destroy both soul and body
in hell. Are not two sparrows sold for a copper coin? And not
one of them falls to the ground apart from the Father's will,
But the very hairs on your head are all numbered. Do not fear
therefore; you are of more value than many sparrows."
(Matthew 10: 28-31)

Jesus simply stated that man can ONLY kill the body, but that's all. Do not fear man, but fear only God. God can destroy the body and soul, but He loves you so much that He even knows the number of hairs on your head! If He chooses to give you that kind of love and attention, why would you allow someone to hinder your relationship and destiny with Him? Man can rape and molest your physical body which is flesh. Your flesh is not going to last forever, but he can't touch your SPIRITUAL body, which is your SOUL. It is eternal and will live forever! God didn't give man the ability or right to touch your soul! Thank God for that! While you may have felt powerless and that it was beyond your control to stop someone from raping, molesting or committing an act of incest or divorcing the PHYSICAL YOU, you have all the power and control to not allow anyone to rape, molest, commit incest or divorce the SPIRITUAL YOU! That power belongs only to you and God!

Jesus also put the flesh issue into perspective for his disciples:

'It is the spirit who gives life; the flesh profits nothing. The
words that I speak to you are spirit, and they are life.'
(John: 6: 63)

'For as the body without the spirit is dead.'
(James 2: 26)

Jesus is telling you not to get so wrapped up in what happens to the physical body; it's merely filthy flesh, and will die anyway, but be more concerned about your SPIRIT, for this is where *life* is. The body carries your spirit, also called your "Soul," while it's on the earth. Once its use and purpose has been fulfilled, it will pass away and your spirit will return to God. I'm not saying neglect your body, for it is the Temple of God and you must take care of it, what I am saying is don't get so distraught over something someone did to it or you.

Keep in mind the fact that your PAST does not determine your future, so therefore REJOICE! Regardless of what has happened to you, it's not over until God says it's over; your best days are ahead of you not behind you. King Solomon, David's son, whom God granted exceptional wisdom, wrote:

> *The end of a thing is better than its beginning; the patient in spirit is better than the proud in spirit. Do not hasten in your spirit to be angry, For anger rests in the bosom of fools. Do not say, "Why were the former days better than these?" For you do not inquire wisely concerning this.*
>
> *(Ecclesiastes 7: 8-10)*

What has happened in your life up to this point, no matter how tragic or traumatic, does not and should not determine how you live today. There are many people who have overcome tremendous adversity who have gone on and become productive in their careers, jobs, businesses, churches, families and lives. They decided to make their latter days better than their former days and give themselves a new start. You can too. Don't get bitter, get better! Don't allow anyone or anything to rob you of the joy that is rightfully yours today! Release It! Consider these notable people who have dealt with their PAST and overcome them and have gone on to lead wonderful, productive and inspiring lives:

Oprah Winfrey- Television and print media empire builder- raped at thirteen, attacked by a cousin, became pregnant, later had a miscarriage....

Tyler Perry- Successful, award winning playwright, writer, director, actor-suffered childhood abuse, attempted suicide to escape his situation....

Donnie McClurkin- Minister and award winning gospel artist-molested by an uncle at the age of thirteen abused and neglected early in life...

PHYSICAL PAST- Medical illness, physical handicap

Some people have physical Giants that hinder and threaten their self-esteem and self-worth. Illnesses and medical conditions can take a tremendous toll on your psyche. The stresses they add to your way of life, your family or your personal and professional life is great at times. I have heard some people say that their illness is a result of God punishing them for some past sin; nothing could be further for the truth. God heals! Although an illness or medical condition can seem to wreak havoc on your life, you have to put it in the proper perspective.

I can personally relate to fighting this Giant and the psychological affect it can have on you. About twenty years ago I suddenly began experiencing some excruciating stomach pains that seemed to occur daily; finally after trying to deal with it with over the counter medications, I decided to go to the doctor to find out what was happening to me. My doctor diagnosed me with having an ulcer and prescribed ulcer medication to address it. I thought, "Ulcer," I'm too young to have an ulcer; besides, ulcers are for "Old" people! Anyway, I took the ulcer medication, but it didn't seem to be working after about a month. Then one day while I was in New Orleans for a getaway, the pain I was having continued, so much so that I cut my trip short and went home to Tennessee and immediately called my doctor to set up an emergency appointment. Fortunately my regular doctor wasn't available, he would have just given me more ulcer medication and sent me home, but his partner was on call and agreed to see me on a Sunday. When I met with him, he stated that the area in which I was having pain was not common for an ulcer so he referred me to a gastroenterology specialist for a series of tests and x-rays.

When I arrived at the facility where the tests were to be conducted, I was in so much pain that when the tests were over, the specialist suggested that I be admitted into the hospital to be monitored while they waited for the results of the tests. Well, come to find out, it wasn't an ulcer at all. I had a form of an intestinal degenerative disorder called Crohn's disease. I thought, "Crohn's disease? What the heck is Crohn's disease?" Neither I nor anyone I knew had ever heard of it before. It didn't matter, the doctor said I had it and that there was no known cure. I thought, 'What I am going to do now?' I had just recently gotten promoted to one of the highest levels in my company where I was responsible for running a whole new group of sales and marketing people; I just had a new baby, bought my first house and now this? Giants! Giants! Giants!

In the weeks and months that followed, I tried to put on a happy front in my office, but the stress of having to change my diet to a bland diet, which meant I could not eat anything I cared for and therefore I was beginning to lose weight (I wasn't that big to start with) while still experiencing the pain of the disease. Add to this the feelings of guilt because I was now in this new position I had worked so hard for with people looking to me for leadership, and yet there were days when I couldn't even get out of bed for the pain. The only medication the disease would respond to was prednisone steroids, which weren't good for me either when you consider its side effects. Due to my intestines not being able to absorb enough of the medication to ease the pain, I had to be placed on a high dosage of it just so a small amount could be absorbed into my system to give me some relief. Mentally and physically this was taking a toll on me and dragging me down. Finally, I decided that I would have a talk with God about it, because obviously He "put" me in this situation for a reason and I needed to know what it was. One day as I was telling God about my life and how uncomfortable this whole ordeal was and how I needed Him to heal me from it, He answered me. His answer was certainly NOT what I wanted to hear or even thought I would hear from Him. It is the same message He tells me today whenever I want to have a pity party when something gets challenging or seems like it is too hard to deal with. He said to me:

"SON, I AM NOT CONCERNED ABOUT YOUR COMFORT!"

I thought; WHAT? He said it again to my spirit, "I AM NOT CONCERNED ABOUT YOUR COMFORT!" Afterwards, there was a feeling of bewilderment that went through me, and I started thinking about what I felt God was saying to me. What did He mean, "He was not concerned about my comfort?" He is supposed to be concerned about my comfort, He's God! What's up with that? Growing up, all I had heard from my grandmother, my mother and the church folks singing about was how God is love and how He would be there whenever I needed Him, so why is He saying that? I thought he was supposed to help me when I called on Him. That's what folks were always saying about Him, and now He is telling me He wasn't concerned about my comfort?

Then I heard Him complete what He was saying, He said:

"SON, I AM NOT CONCERNED ABOUT YOUR COMFORT! I AM CONCERNED ABOUT YOUR CAPABILITY!"

WOW! I was floored, confused, dumbfounded and curious as to what He meant. He went on to say:

"I have loved you and have been there for you all of your life. I gave you the parents and grandparents I gave you because I love you, I gave you the upbringing I gave you because I love you. I gave you the wife and children I gave you because I love you. It's not that I don't love you and that I am not concerned about your comfort, I am, but it is because I made you capable of doing much more than you will EVER be comfortable doing. And I have something greater for you to do, and it will not always be comfortable. I never promised you comfort, I promised you a COMFORTER-THE HOLY GHOST-who can SEE you through anything I PUT you through! My GRACE is sufficient to sustain you!"

God went on to say, "I have never chosen a man to do a work great or small where I considered his comfort to do the task OVER his capability to do it! What you are capable of achieving will always exceed what you are comfortable doing! Consider Abraham who was uncomfortable when I told him to leave everything and everyone he had known in his life behind and to follow me not knowing where he was going, and though he thought his body was dead and he would forever be childless, I made him **capable** of spawning a perpetual civilization, or Moses, who was embarrassed to even speak, yet I made him **capable** of mightily being able to speak to Pharaoh saying "Let My people go" and he led a nation under generational bondage out of Egypt, or Paul, who persecuted my people, yet I made him **capable** of changing, and under tremendous persecution and trials, he become one of my greatest mouthpieces for a new generation."

As the days passed, God began to show me that I was always capable of doing something about my situation, comfortable or not. So are you! If you are dealing with a medical or illness Giant, I suggest you consider doing what He told me to do about my situation as well. God had something greater for me to do in my life, but He had to condition me to not always look at the *obstacles,* but to focus on the *opportunities.* As He said, "He makes us capable of achieving far more than we will ever be comfortable doing," and He gives us opportunities each day to improve our outlook and rise to a higher level. He asked me, 'Are you capable of opening your eyes to see the beautiful sunshine I have given you this day?' Check, I can do that! 'Are you capable of smiling and warmly greeting the nurses and visitors when then come to check on you?' Check, I can do that! 'Are you capable of opening your mouth and praying to Me when you aren't feeling your best?' Check, I can do that! 'Are you capable of trusting Me even when you don't know how or if I am going to heal you?' Check, I can do that! I think you get the gist of how the rest of the story went.

Here's an example of how trust and faithfulness in God works. When I began to have a better attitude about my situation, and began to be friendlier towards the nursing and medical staff that took care of me, not only did many of them become my friends, but some became clients as well, and also a great source for referrals for me throughout the hospital and the medical community. As I started focusing on how blessed and loved I was and not on the illness that was in my body, I began to have a greater appreciation for the fact that I was STILL alive! I could function, and that I could go to God with anything that bothered me, regardless of how big or small, He would listen.

Needless to say God went on to heal me, but even if He hadn't I would have been ok with it, because I discovered His GRACE is sufficient to see me through any challenge that any Giant throws my way, and so will you. If you are dealing with a physical or medical Giant, first of all don't get discouraged or lose hope. Tell Him about it. He's listening! Even if God doesn't heal you, just know it is not the end of your world, but perhaps it's a new beginning. God is not punishing you for something you've done in your past, He doesn't play games or tricks on you like that, but maybe He is trying to get you to see things differently. Perhaps He's getting you to realize that you are capable of accomplishing much more than you have up to this point in your life, and He is preparing you for a greater journey. There might be someone watching you who will be encouraged and inspired by your story and how you choose to deal with this challenge. God never does anything without a **purpose**, a **process** and a **promise**. The *purpose* is to get the 'Glory from your story,' the *process* is to 'condition you for the journey,' and the *promise* is 'to sustain you as you go through it.' You may not see His purpose in the beginning, and the process may be uncomfortable right now, but know for sure you can count on His promise to sustain you during the process.

FINANCIAL PAST-foreclosure, auto repossession, bankruptcy, business or financial failure

Bank bailouts, frozen credit, stimulus packages, record deficits, record unemployment, record bankruptcies, plant closings, corporate downsizings...where does it end? The news headlines are constantly bombarding us with these doom and gloom scenarios of life as we will have to get to know it in the future. It's enough to paralyze you and make you want to throw in the towel, throw your hands up asking, "What's the use of trying to get ahead when everything seems to be going down like never before?" Does the frustration of thinking that there just aren't any good jobs out there anymore or that you might lose the one you have and nobody's hiring discourage you? Yet it seems every day you hear about these bank executives and corporate CEOs taking all of our tax dollars and using it for their own selfish and self-indulgent desires with reckless abandon, and the government seems to want to keep giving them more money with little or no accountability, yet you and those around are suffering like never before. You might be asking, "Where's my bailout, where's my stimulus package?" Have you had to declare bankruptcy, had an automobile repossessed, foreclosure, business failure recently or in the past? Perhaps you are experiencing one or more of these situations today. Financial Giants can affect your ability to function properly and enjoy today. You may feel like you've failed to protect your family from the uncertainty of the times we're in.

Once, David faced a similar financial PAST that shook his confidence, which resulted in the loss of his family and all of his possessions. This potentially devastating loss occurred after he defeated the giant Goliath-which is usually the way Giants (life situations) are; it seems once you finish defeating one, there seems to be another one just around the corner waiting to pounce on you. You can never get so discourage by the events in your life that you give up trying, or let your guard down even after a great victory. After

David's great victory over Goliath, he became so distraught from being constantly chased and threatened by Saul that he decided the only way he could be safe would be to join the Philistines (the enemy):

> *And David said in his heart, "Now I shall perish someday by the hand of Saul. There is nothing better for me than that I should speedily escape to the land of the Philistines." Then David arose and went over with the six hundred men who were with him to Achish the king of Gath (Gath is a Philistine city).*
>
> *(1 Samuel; 27: 1-2)*

Can you believe it? How crazy was that, David and his army joining forces with the Philistines because of his FEAR and his PAST? Unfortunately, that's what happens sometimes when you let your mind and thinking get out of control. Logic and rationale tend to get tossed out of the window and you irrationally react to the pressure of the situation and often bring something worse upon yourself than what you were facing to begin with. Can you relate? Maybe you've made an irrational decision based on the events in your life. I have a very dear friend who gave me some of the most valuable advice I have been given that has served me well in moments like these. I use it almost on a weekly, if not certainly a monthly basis. I suggest you consider it when you are faced with a tough decision.

It goes like this:

"Never make a permanent decision based on a temporary situation."

In other words, 'troubles don't last always,' so don't make permanent decisions that you may regret later concerning a temporary condition. The situation or event is not going to last forever. Some decisions cannot be easily reversed, such as words SPOKEN in the heat of the moment cannot be taken back! This piece of advice has served me well and has stopped me from making some decisions that would have been very costly to me later on. I may have gotten some temporary relief from the pressing issue, but looking back, it would not have worked in my favor in the long run. Financial pressures tend to make you speak and act irrationally and it can cost you much more later. There are financial predators that prey on people in financial distress; predatory lenders, title loan companies, check cashing outfits, all kinds of shady operators whose objective is to get you further in financial bondage and distress. Stay away from these kinds of Giants. If you are already in their snares, work to get from under their grip as soon as possible.

When David acted irrationally in this temporary situation, he lost everything! He became the chief guardian for the king, King Achish of Gath-a Philistine, which meant David might have to fight against his own people one day - the nation of Israel, a possibility he may not have given much thought to at the time. David's plan was to fight the other nations that were enemies of both Israel and the Philistines, therefore avoiding a direct confrontation with Israel. When he defeated one of these nations, he would kill all the men and women of the land, so there would be no one left to tell the king what really happened. Then he would take all of the goods and livestock back to King Achish.

When King Achish would question him about where he raided that day, he would tell him that it was one of the villages of Israel. This charade went on for a while. Then one day the Philistines, as was their custom, gathered all of their armies together at a city called Aphek for a pass and review of their troops before the lords of the Philistines. During the processional, David and his men were spotted marching with King Achish's army. One of the princes of the Philistines inquired as to what were those Hebrews doing here, and is this not David, of whom they sang in their dances saying; "Saul has slain his thousands, and David his ten thousands?" But, King Achish tried to tell them that David had been loyal to him and that he really had changed to their side, but they were hearing none of it, and immediately demanded that he send David back to be with his people.

So David and his men returned to Ziklag, the Philistine village where they had been staying, only to find that while they were gone, the Amalekites came in and invaded the southern region of the land of the Philistines, which included Ziklag, burned their camp, took their wives and children captive and carried off all their goods! When David and his men saw what had happened, they lifted up their voices and wept until they could weep no more:

> *So David and his men returned to the city, and there it was, burned with fire; and their wives, their sons, and their daughters had been taken captive. Then David and the people who were with him lifted up their voices and wept, until they had no more power to weep. And David's two wives, Ahinoam, the Jezreelitess, and Abigail the widow of Nabel the Carmelite, had been taken captive. Now David was greatly distressed, for the people spoke of stoning him, because the soul of all the people was grieved, every man for his sons and his daughters.*
>
> *(1 Samuel 30: 3-6)*

Can you imagine? EVERYTHING, GONE! Wives gone, children gone, gated community house burned down, Escalade gone, Lexus gone, Mercedes gone, business gone, bank accounts wiped out, friends ready to stone you, because not only did you lose YOUR stuff, but you caused them to lose THEIRS TOO, following YOU! Maybe you have been there before or you are there now. Like David you were WIPED OUT! What do you do now? How do you battle the Giant of a Financial PAST where you have lost EVERYTHING?

So, what did David do? Let's see:

> *But David STRENGTHENED HIMSELF in the Lord his God. Then David said to Abaithar the priest, "Please bring the ephod here to me." So David INQUIRED OF THE LORD, saying, "Shall I pursue this troop? Shall I overtake them?" And HE answered him, "Pursue, for you shall SURELY overtake them and WITHOUT FAIL recover all."*
>
> *(1 Samuel 30: 6-8)*

Hallelujah! First David *strengthened* himself (the KJV says, "He ENCOURAGED Himself") in the Lord his God, and he sought God directly. Did you get that? Before David did anything, he encouraged himself and showed reverence to the Lord His God! That's where it begins. No matter what has happened, BEFORE you do ANYTHING-before you get angry, revengeful, discouraged, upset, fearful, wanting to set someone straight, take illegal or immoral actions, or before making any move, you must find a way to seek the Lord your God and encourage yourself in Him! I know it will be tough, but you don't just want to get a result, you want to get the RIGHT result!

Here are the steps David took to bring about the RIGHT result:

FIRST- ENCOURAGE YOURSELF IN THE LORD: Get off to yourself, pray and lift your heart and your voice to God. It may not seem like it at the time, nor will you feel like it necessarily, but you still have the ability to have peace in the middle of your storm regardless of what your storm is. The best way to do this is to go to Psalms and find some scriptures that tells you what David said to encourage himself. Here are some to start with that have helped me:

> But You, O Lord, are a shield for me, My glory and the One who lifts up my head. I cried to the Lord with my voice, And He heard me from His holy hill.
>
> *(Psalm 3: 3-4)*

> You have put gladness in my heart, More than in the season that their grain and wine increased. I will both lie down in peace, and sleep; For You alone, O Lord make me dwell in safety.
>
> *(Psalm 4: 7-8)*

> I will love You, O Lord, my strength. The Lord is my rock and my fortress and my deliverer; My God, my strength, in whom I will trust; My shield and the horn of my salvation, my stronghold. I will call upon the Lord, who is worthy to be praised; So shall I be saved from my enemies.
>
> *(Psalm 18: 1-3)*

The Lord is my light and my salvation; Whom shall I fear? The Lord is the strength of my life; Of whom shall I be afraid? When the wicked came against me to eat up my flesh, My enemies and foes, They stumbled and fell. Though an army may encamp against me, MY HEART SHALL NOT FEAR; Though war may rise against me, In this I will be confident.

(Psalm 27: 1-3)

One thing I have desired of the Lord, That will I seek: That I may dwell in the house of the Lord all the days of my life, To behold the beauty of the Lord, And to inquire in His temple.

(Psalm 27: 4)

Cast your burdens on the Lord, And He shall sustain you; He shall never permit the righteous to be moved.

(Psalm 55: 22)

David strengthened himself in what he knew his God could do. He didn't give priority to his situation; he gave priority to his God! Neither did he dwell on the place where he found himself; his first focus was on the Lord and His grace and ability. When you face a crossroad and you need to get some direction as to what to do next, dwell in the word and salvation of God first. Strengthen and encourage yourself in the Lord. Don't seek comfort from people, they can only "soothe" you and offer temporary relief, but only God can "solve" your problem.

SECOND- GET IN THE RIGHT POSITION TO ADDRESS GOD: You may ask, what do you mean get in the right position to address God? Note that David asked Abiathar, the Priest, to "bring the ephod here to me." In God's law and Israelite culture, only the priest was allowed to talk to God directly. God spoke to the king and the people through the priest. To show reverence and respect, the high priest wore an ephod, which is a sacred garment worn by a 'High priest' in their attempt to gain insight into a question or situation by way of a standardized process or ritual when talking to God. David understood this; therefore, he asked that the ephod be brought to him so that he could approach God for himself, and not through the priest. David needed to talk to God directly, so he asked the priest for the ephod to wear. Your Giant may be something that you need to take directly to God. There's nothing your pastor, bishop, husband, wife, child, father, mother, brother, sister, uncle, aunt, cousin, homeboy, home girl, ace, road dog, physic, palm reader, frat brother, sorority sister, co-worker or anyone else can tell you about how to resolve or deal with this problem. This was one of those times for David. Maybe you've consulted some or all of these people in the past, but not this time. Even though we don't have to wear ephods or go through a High Priest to approach God, there is still a proper to do it.

You may be thinking irrationally right now. This Giant is messing with your head and your thoughts, as I said earlier, these Giants are psychological. Even though you may not be thinking straight about the situation right now, you don't want to make the mistake of improperly approaching God and start making demands, threats and throwing questions at Him like, "How could You let this happen to me?" "When are You going to do something?" "Why didn't You stop this from happening to me?" No, No, No! Be careful how you address the Lord your God like David was! God is fully aware of your situation, yet He doesn't owe you an explanation for anything He does or doesn't do for you. You must first have reverence and respect for WHO He is and HOW to properly access Him.

David also knew that he was dealing with a Giant that affected the lives of the men who were loyal and followed him, and he needed to hear from God for their sake as well. Normally kings would have to go to the high priest to inquire of God about what to do, and the priest would get an answer and relay it back to the king, but this was too critical and important for David to allow anyone else to speak to God about on his behalf. David wanted clarity and to have direct access to God himself, and he sought it properly.

We have direct access to God too. It's through **Jesus Christ**! He is our 'High Priest' who gives us a direct line of communication and access to God! We don't have to go through anyone or anything else-no ephods, rituals, middlemen, preachers, gatekeepers or any of those things, just Jesus:

> *Seeing then that we have a great High Priest who has passed through the heavens, Jesus the Son of God, let us hold fast our confession. For we do not have a High Priest who cannot sympathize with our weaknesses, but was in all points tempted as we are, YET WITHOUT SIN. Let us therefore come BOLDLY to the throne of grace, that we may obtain mercy and find grace to help in the time of need.*
> (Hebrews 4: 14-16)

> *Jesus said to him, "I am the way, the truth, and the life. No one comes to the Father except through Me."*
> (John 14: 6)

Isn't it wonderful that we can have clarity and direct access to God through Jesus Christ? Jesus gives us direct access to God the Father to have our petitions heard:

> *"Most assuredly, I say to you, he who believes in Me, the works that I do he will do also and greater works than these he will do, because I go to My Father. And WHATEVER you ask in My name, that will I do, that the Father may be glorified in the Son. If you ask ANYTHING in My name, I will do it."*
> (John 14: 12-14)

Jesus **guarantees** us access! ***"If you ask ANYTHING in My name, I WILL DO IT!"*** It doesn't get any plainer than that!

THIRD- INQUIRE OF HIS DIRECTION: Even though David was upset, distraught, hurt and confused, he held his emotions in check and inquired of God for direction. He didn't just react out of his desires, fears or distress. David was smart about how he sought an answer from God. He understood that to communicate with God, he needed to be SPECIFIC with his inquiry. He did not allow his emotional state to cause him to go to God rambling and babbling on about something that was not clear. ***A direct answer to direct questions is how God communicates with us.***

How about you? When you inquire or request something of God are you specific about it? Are your requests *clear, concise, and direct?* Have you inquired or requested something of God and have yet to receive an answer? Perhaps you should consider HOW you are making your request.

David asked God two SPECIFIC questions. His first question was a question of DIRECTION and the second was a question of PROMISE:

FIRST QUESTION- "Shall I pursue this troop?" In other words, 'Should I go after them?'

David inquired of the Lord, saying, "Shall I pursue this troop?" David asked the Lord what he should do. Now it may have been that David wanted to attack them all along, BUT he sought God's direction and blessing FIRST before he made any move. David knew that if God told him WHAT to do and promised him success if he did it, then there was no way he could lose because GOD COULD NOT LIE. There is no doubt in my mind had God told David not to pursue them, and to go in another direction, he would have done so. David trusted in the Lord his God enough to know that God always had his best interest at heart and that He would never have him do something that was not for his good.

SECOND QUESTION-"Shall I overtake them?" In other words, 'Will You help me conquer them?'

"Shall I overtake them" was not a question of doubt, but one of divine protection and promise. He knew that God was more than able to deliver on whatever He promised! If God promised him the result, the victory was his! David began to elevate his relationship with God with this encounter. He had lost everything and he went back to the source of all things good- God. It didn't matter what the situation was, or how grim the circumstance, David knew 'if God was in it, he would win it!'

By developing the same attitude, mindset and trust towards God that David had, you too can and will move past the Financial Giants you are facing and get on the path of recovery knowing that your success is GUARANTEED. God always has YOUR best interest in His heart! Like David, seek His direction and plan of action; do not be tempted to rely on your own desires, solutions, whims or understanding.

FOURTH- WAIT ON HIS ANSWER: After David inquired of the Lord about what he should do and asked if he would bless him, he waited for God to answer him! Although waiting is not always easy, in many cases it's necessary. You need to be clear that you have heard from God. Unfortunately this is where we tend to make the biggest mistake and begin to mess things up worse because of our IMPATIENCE!

Impatience has destroyed more lives, marriages, families, relationships, businesses, successes, children, careers, plans, dreams and hopes than anything else in this life. I know it is not easy waiting, especially with the Giants knocking at the door; the bill collectors harassing you with those annoying phone calls, collection company threats, foreclosure notices, repo man in the driveway, children's college threatening to kick them out if they don't get the tuition, you have the layoff notice, or termination papers in your hand, it goes on and on, what do you do?

The problem is you think you can't wait, because your **PAST** (Psychological Act Suspending your Today's) has caught up with you! You think you must act now, so you make some hastily conspired, ill conceived plans, and you go off and do something that was not directed or blessed by God, and then you expect Him to go along with it anyway because He saw you were in need but He didn't move fast enough for you and......NOT!

GOD IS NOT MOVED BY YOUR NEED!

Let me say this again, *"God is not moved by your need!"*

GOD IS MOVED BY YOUR SEED!

Are you planting *"good seed?"* In this case your *seed* is your "FAITH!" Your faith must be planted in God's word and His ability to deliver on what He promises! David had his faith planted solidly in God's word and His promises. His need would not have mattered had he not had the faith to believe that God could deliver on whatever He promised, and the patience to wait on Him to do it:

> *But without FAITH it is IMPOSSIBLE to please Him, for he who comes to God MUST believe that He is, and that He is a rewarder of those who diligently seek Him.*
>
> *(Hebrews 11: 6)*

This is where it begins. In order to receive ANYTHING from God, you must FIRST believe that He exists! Notice the scripture says "For he who comes to God, must BELIEVE that HE IS." If you don't believe that He is, what's the use of calling upon Him? If you didn't think that someone had the ability to do what you needed done, why would you ask them? Also, if you've ever wondered why God didn't answer you when you called upon Him to help get you out of a situation you got yourself into and it seemed like you were about to lose it all, it's likely that God wasn't in your decision to move forward and take that action, YOU WERE! Those were not HIS plans, they were YOURS! You trusted in yourself to achieve a result, not God! God will not bless something that He did not tell you to do, or promised you would succeed. Why would you expect Him to? Because you are desperate and impatient is not a reason for God to act on your behalf. You must have your seed of FAITH planted in His word and WAIT for Him to answer you according to His will, and in His own time, not yours!

FAITH is God's "CURRENCY" and it is your means of payment to obtain WHATEVER you need from Him! Anything is yours if you pay the price of faith to believe in Him and that He will grant your request, but you must wait on Him to give it to you. He will respond in His own time and in His own way. Bank on it!

> *And when the disciples saw it, they marveled, saying, "How did the fig tree wither away so soon?" So Jesus answered and said to them, "Assuredly, I say to you, if you have faith and DO NOT DOUBT, you will not only do what was done to the fig tree, but also if you say to this mountain, Be removed and be cast into the sea,' IT WILL BE DONE. And WHATEVER things you ask in prayer, BELIEVING, you will receive."*
> *(Matthew 21: 21-22)*

David had true FAITH and belief in God, and he WAITED for God to answer him. He believed God was able to deliver on what He promised, and sure enough, God answered David:

> *And HE answered him, "PURSUE, for you shall SURELY OVERTAKE THEM, and **WITHOUT FAIL** RECOVER ALL."*
> *(1 Samuel 30: 8)*

Hallelujah! Did you see that? David waited on God to answer him and when He did He did so with instructions, directions, and a promise of success! I truly think that David would not have made any move until he heard from God! He would have remained standing right there in the rubble of what used to be his house; with his wives gone, children gone, Escalade gone, Lexus gone, Mercedes gone, bank accounts gone, it didn't matter. He would have remained right there understanding like Job understood:

> *"Naked I came from my mother's womb, And naked shall I return there. The Lord gave, and the Lord has taken away; Blessed be the name of the Lord." In all this Job did not sin nor charge God with wrong.*
> *(Job 1: 21-22)*

Whatever God decided would have been fine with David. If God had answered David and told him go to another city and start over, David would have. David knew that everything he had acquired came from God. He, like you, had nothing when he came into this world, and he would carry nothing out of it. If God gave it to him and decided to take it away, that was alright, too. Blessed be the name of the Lord!

How about you? Will you wait on God to answer you and accept His answer whatever it may be? Will you be patient and not make a move until you hear from Him? After David received his answer from God, he then pursued the Amalekites with four hundred of his chosen men who also lost their family and goods. David had six hundred fighting men, but only four hundred went with him to recover their families and goods. The other two hundred stayed behind because they were too weary and distraught, they could not even cross the brook, so they stayed behind to protect what was left of the camp. When David and his men set out to find the Amalekites, God arranged it so that they would come upon a man, an Egyptian, who was a servant of an Amalekite who had taken ill and his master left him behind to die. He told David all about how they invaded their land and took their families and possessions, and that he could lead them directly to the Amalekite camp where the men were. David fed and took care of the man until he regained his strength. When the Egyptian regained his strength, he led them to where the Amalekites were camped.

When David and his men approached the camp of the Amalekites, they found them in the middle of celebrating their great conquest and were spread out all over the land, eating, drinking and dancing because of all the great spoil which had been taken from the land of the Philistines and Judah. Then David ATTACKED them. He launched his attack from sun up till sun down until there was not a man standing and David recovered all that the Amalekites had carried away, just like God said he would. This Giant, the Amalekites, didn't stand a chance against David and God's promise of victory. Not a hair on David's wives or children was harmed. All of his belongings and property was recovered. David lacked nothing, just like God promised. Not only did David recover all that was taken from him, but he also took the flocks, herds and livestock of the Amalekites which was called, "David's spoils:"

> So David recovered all that the Amalekites had carried away, and David rescued his two wives. And nothing of theirs was lacking, either small or great, sons or daughters, spoil or anything which they had taken from them; David recovered all.
> (1 Samuel 30: 18-19)

David had been with the Philistines for a year and four months before this happened and afterwards he came to his senses. Unfortunately it took a tragedy like this to bring him around to remembering WHO he was, WHOSE he was and WHERE his true help comes from. Regardless of what it took to bring him to his senses, he was able to ATTACK HIS GIANT, the right way! He went back to God, his source, for everything he had able to do in his life! He sought instructions from God, and he followed those instructions and directions for recovering everything that was taken from him and then some. He knew God is always faithful to His word.

How will you know God has answered you?

Now you may be asking, **"How will I know that God has answered me? How can I know that He has given me the direction and promise for success?"** You will know it is God, if your answer contains ALL of the following 3 criteria. If it does not contain ALL of them, then it is not of God. One or two out of the three does not count.

You will know your answer is from God if it:

1. GLORIFIES GOD! Will He get the "Glory from the story?"
2. BENEFIT OTHERS! Who besides you will benefit from it?
3. CHANGES YOU! Will you be any different as a result of it?

Your answer will contain these three criteria if it is from God. When David received his answer from God, it contained the three criteria described above. Then and only then did he make a move.

1. **God got the glory**-David gave all credit for the victory to God.

When David and the four hundred fighting men returned with all of the spoils from the victory to rejoin the other two hundred men whom they had left at the Brook Besor, the men who had gone and fought with David were upset because he wanted to share the spoils with the two hundred. They felt that the two hundred deserved to get their family and goods back, but not share in the spoils.

But David said to them:

> *"My brethren, you shall not do so with* **what the Lord has given us, who has preserved us and delivered into our hand the troop that came against us.** *For who will heed you in this matter?"*
> *(1 Samuel 30: 23-24)*

David gave the Lord his God the credit for the victory, even when his men wanted to lay claim to the spoils and keep it for themselves and not share it with the others! David would not keep any of it. He felt the credit belonged to the Lord and who were they to deny anyone anything of His?

2. **David's people and the surrounding lands benefited.**

When David recovered all that belonged to him and took the spoils of the Amalekites, he didn't keep them for himself. He gave them to the people who fought with him and those who had helped him in his life. He gave some to the elders of Judah, and some to the cities and towns that sheltered him as he escaped Saul's pursuit. They were given the spoils of the victory equally:

> *But as his part is who goes down to the battle, so shall his part be who stays by the supplies; they shall share alike. So it was, from that day forward; he made it a statue and an ordinance for Israel TO THIS DAY. Now when David came to Ziklag,* **he sent some of the spoil to the elders of Judah, to his friends, saying, "Here is a present for you from the spoil of the enemies**

of the Lord."....*and all the places where David himself and his men were accustomed to rove.*

(1 Samuel 30: 24-26, 31)

3. David was changed.

David left the Philistine army and went back to his people with a greater reliance and dependence on God to guide and protect him. From that point on, David consulted with God about everything, and he was also permitted to make his inquires directly to God. He would need it, because shortly thereafter, Saul was killed in a battle with the Philistines, along with his sons Jonathan, Abinadab and Malchishua. There were no heirs left in Saul's house, and David would soon become the king of the unified house of Judah with the nation of Israel:

> *Now the time that David dwelt in the country of the Philistines was one full year and four months.*
>
> *(1 Samuel 27: 7)*

After David heard of Saul's death, he inquired of God about what to do next. Through the trials with Saul, the Philistines and his own personal challenges, God had prepared David to reign as the king of a reunified Israel:

> *It happened after this that David inquired of the Lord, saying, "Shall I go up to any of the cities of Judah?" And the Lord said to him, "Go up." David said, "Where shall I go up?" And He said, "To Hebron." Then the men of Judah came, and there they anointed David king over the house of Judah.*
>
> *(2 Samuel 2: 1, 4)*

> *Then all the tribes of Israel came to David at Hebron and spoke, saying, "Indeed we are your bone and your flesh." Therefore all the elders of Israel came to the king at Hebron, and King David made a covenant with them at Hebron before the Lord. And they anointed David king over Israel.*
>
> *(2 Samuel 5: 1, 3)*

When you receive your answer from God after a devastating loss or major disruption to your way of life, you will also notice a distinct difference between how you respond to challenges now versus how you handled them before. Your choices will be more deliberate, thoughtful and sound. You won't be as hasty, panicky and tempted to look for the quick fix this time around. Wait on God to answer you; in due time He will, and you will be able to "recover all" in record time while being a blessing to others in the process.

MENTAL PAST- Drug, alcohol or substance abuse, sexual promiscuity and perversion, homosexuality, pornography

These psychological acts of your past are often brought on by you and the choices you've made or your abased desires. These Giants can have a debilitating and humiliating effect on your mind and self esteem. The fear, shame and humiliation you suffer as a result of their existence in your life can be devastating. Drug, alcohol and substance abuse and pervasive sexual desires can lead to all kinds of destructive behaviors which can have you constantly living in bondage like a slave to this past or current behavior. These substances and activities can have a hold on you and grip every fiber of your being. Although they are manifested in the natural through an addiction or habit, they influence your behavior and actions. These demonic spirits also play tricks on your mind (psyche) and emotions.

The first step in dealing with these Giants is recognizing that they exist, and that you want to rid yourself of them for good. **You can't conquer what you won't confront!** Denial only delays the process of getting healed. I know people; star athletes, entertainers and business people, who suffer from addictions who have yet to recognize or admit that they have a problem. They use phrases like, "I can stop whenever I want to," or "It's not that bad," or "Just one last time, then I'll quit"...etc. Only when you recognize that you have a problem, and you truly want to eliminate it from your life will you be compelled to seek the proper and professional help that you need to begin addressing it. Otherwise, you will not be motivated or committed to do what is necessary to change this behavior.

If you have a truly heartfelt, honest and earnest desire to rid yourself of these addictions or habits, then I strongly recommend that you consult a physician or counselor trained in your area of addiction. You may not be able to conquer this on your own, especially in the beginning. If it's drugs, alcohol, sexual or whatever, I suggest that you seek proper attention immediately to address these Giants as you build up your faith, trust, reliance and relationship with God. He will ultimately be the one to help you conquer and defeat this Giant, permanently.

It may seem like these Giants of your PAST have an unshakeable grip on your mind and emotions right now, and you might be thinking you will not be able to kick this habit or addiction, but I declare to you today that you can be free of these demonic spirits. They have kept you off balance and out of sync long enough. These Giants have tricked you into thinking you are not worthy of God's love and help, but they're wrong; He loves you regardless of what you've done, and wants to see you through this. While you seek the help you need to begin conquering this Giant, I strongly encourage you to start changing the behavior that led to you getting caught up in this cycle of destruction and despair in the first place. You can begin your quest right now towards becoming the man or woman God created and intended for you to be-A GIANT SLAYER.

David said in Psalm:

Blessed is the man Who walks not in the counsel of the ungodly, Nor stand in the paths of sinners, Nor sits in the seat of the scornful; But his delight is in the law of the Lord, And in His law he meditates day and night.

(Psalm 1: 1)

You weren't BORN a drug or sex addict, alcoholic, abuser, homosexual or sexually promiscuous person, you picked that up from somewhere or someone at some point in your life, wouldn't you agree? Chances are someone introduced you to this kind of lifestyle. Take a moment and look back at your life and identify the people and influences that led to you getting into this kind of activity. Are these people or influences still in your life today? If so, you need to begin today to get rid of them now. Your journey towards change begins here. You need to get away from the "COUNSEL OF THE **UNGODLY**," immediately! These destructive influences can do nothing for you except keep you in the bondage they are in. A demonic spirit's purpose is to take over the regions, territories, homes, churches, synagogues, temples, neighborhoods, companies and schools that they occupy, and you are in their territory right now doing the things they do. Rather than "meditate" on the things of God, you are meditating on the counsel of the ungodly, and the destructive forces that threaten to keep you held captive.

There's a story in the Bible that illustrates how these destructive forces operate and identifies their purpose. One day after Jesus had finished ministering to the multitude of people who were constantly around Him, he decided to sail with His disciples in a boat to the far side of the river to rest, when suddenly He was met by a man possessed with, 'unclean spirits'. When Jesus questioned the man about his condition, the man's response revealed a lot about how demons operate:

> *And when He had come out of the boat, immediately there met Him out of the tombs a man with an unclean spirit, **who had his dwelling among the tombs:** and no one could bind him... When he saw Jesus, he ran and worshiped Him. And he cried out with a loud voice and said, "What have I to do with You, Jesus, Son to the Most High God? I implore you by God that You do not torment me." For He said to him, "Come out of the man, unclean spirit!" Then He (Jesus) asked him, "What is your name?" And he answered saying, "My name is Legion; for we are many." Also he begged Him earnestly that He would not send them out of the COUNTRY.*
>
> *(Mark 5: 2-3, 6-10)*

A demon's goal is to take over families, communities, regions and territories. Notice in the scripture, this man lived in the tombs, dwelling among the same people in the area who were being tormented just like him. The first thing you have to do in order to begin your road to recovery is to get out of that environment. You cannot fight an addiction by keeping company with the same people who got you hooked on the drugs in the first place, or by staying in the same surroundings you were in when you started this destructive lifestyle! Notice in the scripture that the unclean spirit named Legion, begged Jesus not to send **them** from the country. In other words, this is where they wanted to stay to do their insidious deeds. If you are constantly around the people who have the kind of lifestyle you are trying to get out of, do you really think they will be encouraging you to leave or happy to see you go? No, that's the life they are into so they see nothing wrong with it. You're the one who will have to remove yourself from this environment, whatever the cost.

Also notice that this demon knew WHO Jesus was, "What have I to do with You, Jesus, Son of the Most High God," he said. Demons recognize who Jesus is and they will respond to the utterance of His name and His presence in your life. As you begin to read and study the Bible, and start speaking God's words against your Giants, THEY will respond! They have no choice. They will also try to fight back. These Giants don't want to give up any territory or release a victim, so get ready for a fight. The battle is for control of your mind and body. David spoke with authority to Goliath and told him how it was going to be, not the other way around. You can speak with authority to your Giants, too. Speak to that addiction, habit, disorder. Better yet don't just speak to it... ATTACK IT! Put this Giant of destructive behavior or addiction on notice that you will not allow it to dominate your life any longer. Here are some scriptures you can speak to yourself and to your Giant to remind you of God's supreme power to help you in this time of renewing your mindset:

For You are my rock and my fortress; Therefore, for Your name's sake, Lead me and guide me. Pull me out of the net which they have secretly laid for me, For You are my strength. Into Your hands I commit my spirit; You have redeemed me, O LORD God of truth.

(Psalm 31: 3-5)

For I hear the slander of many; Fear is on every side; While they take counsel together against me, They scheme to take away my life. But as for me, I trust in You, O Lord; I say, "You are my God." My times are in Your hand; Deliver me from my enemies, And from those who persecute me.

(Psalm 31: 13-15)

Be of good COURAGE, and He shall strengthen your heart, All you who hope in the Lord.

(Psalm 31: 24)

If you have gone through a mental PAST like this one, be encouraged. Don't let anyone make you feel guilty for having gone through it. God brought you through this for reasons that only He can reveal and explain to you. Stay in prayer and be receptive to hearing His word. Releasing your mental PAST is an area you can address that will give you the leverage you need to effectively attack and conquer your Giants! When the Giants of your PAST no longer have a stronghold on your emotions, finances, health and mind, then you can move forward with the confidence and assurance of knowing that there is nothing that can come against you that God cannot see you through. The more you learn to rely on Him to help you with the challenges of your PAST, and begin to access His strategies towards living a happy, blessed and highly-favored life, the stronger you will become as a conqueror of the Giants that will come in the future.

Chapter Four

Recount Little VICTORIES!

....."For I know the plans I have for you," declares the Lord, "plans to prosper you and not to harm you, plans to give you hope and a future. Then will you call upon Me and come to Me, and I will listen to you. You will seek Me and find Me when you seek Me with all your heart. I WILL BE FOUND BY YOU," declares the Lord.

(Jeremiah 29: 11-14 NIV)

"When you are in any contest you should work as if there were to the very last minute, a chance to lose it."

Dwight Eisenhower

If you want to know that God has proven himself to be on your side and that you can attack and defeat the Giants you face, simply look back at the victories God has already brought you through like David did. Build on these past victories no matter how big or small. Recount the times you've faced a challenge and came through it. Something as small as getting a good parking spot at the market can be seen as God showing you favor. Use any incident you can as a great example of God giving you the victory in a challenge.

When word got back to Saul that David was going to fight Goliath, Saul's inquiry to David in essence was to say, 'Are you crazy?'

And Saul said to David, "You are not able to go against this Philistine to fight with him; for you are a youth, and he a man of war from his youth."

(1 Samuel 17: 33)

Saul thought David had taken leave of his senses. "You, a youth, fight a giant who has been fighting since his youth?" 'Are you out of your mind?' However, David wasn't operating OUT of his mind; he was operating IN his FAITH:

> *But David said to Saul, "Your servant used to keep his father's sheep, and when a lion or a bear came and took a lamb out of the flock, I went out after it and struck it, and delivered the lamb from its mouth; and when it arose against me, I caught it by its beard, and struck and killed it. Your servant has killed both lion and bear; and this uncircumcised Philistine will be like one of them, seeing he has defied the armies of the living God." Moreover David said, "The Lord who delivered me from the paw of the lion and from the paw of the bear, He will deliver me from the hand of this Philistine."*
>
> *(1 Samuel 17: 34-37)*

David recounted all of the times when God had delivered him in the past. He had total faith and belief that God would protect him and give him the victory over this "uncircumcised Philistine," because He had done so in the past against a lion and a bear that threatened the sheep. David magnified in his mind the purpose and meaning of these victories. This gave him the courage to face up to this challenge with the confidence and assurance to know that Goliath would meet the same fate. The thought never entered his mind that he wouldn't be victorious over the giant.

In the book of Psalm, David gives us a glimpse into his communication and relationship to God. I encourage you to consider adopting David's perspective of God as your protector:

> *I will love You, O Lord, my strength. The Lord is my rock and fortress and my deliverer; My God, my strength, in whom I will trust; My shield and the horn of my salvation, my stronghold. I will call upon the Lord, who is worthy to be praised; so shall I be saved from my enemies.*
>
> *(Psalm 18: 1-3)*

For by You I can run against a troop, By my God I can leap over a wall. As for God, His way is perfect; The word of the Lord is proven; He is a shield to all who trust Him.

(Psalm 18: 28-30)

The Lord is the light of my salvation; Whom shall I fear? The Lord is the strength of my life; of whom shall I be afraid? When the wicked came against me to eat up my flesh, My enemies and foes, They stumbled and fell, Though an army may encamp against me, My heart shall not fear; Though war may rise against me, In this I will be confident.

(Psalm 27: 1-3)

You can see that David had total faith and trust in the Lord his God to deliver him through whatever came against him, seen or unseen. How about you? Are there some small victories God has delivered you from that you can build upon? Maybe you received some money that came at just the right time, or perhaps you saw an ad in the paper for a job that you applied for and got, or even though you had no degree or experience, you got a position that required one or both. Can you recount a time in school you aced an exam that you didn't think you could pass? What about the time you survived the car accident and walked away with little more than a scratch, or turned around at just the right moment to avoid an accident? What did you feel when that moment happened? Joy, calm, peace, love, protected, lead by something you couldn't explain? If you look hard and long enough you can probably recall many times like these. Times I call "*moments of deliverance*" when God showed you that He will protect you and carry you through to victory by having done so in the past. Build upon these moments. Sit down right now and recount some of those times, instances, moments of triumph, situations of salvation. We all have had them. Praise God for them.

Get out a piece of paper and write them down, NOW! Don't let this moment pass. Confirm God's presence and His hand of protection in your life. Regardless of how small or insignificant you thought the victory might have been, write it down. When you do this, you begin to see the pattern of victories God has given you throughout your life. Unfortunately, most people only focus on the things that didn't work out or the times when they lost something, and they magnify these incidents instead. This only puts you in a downward spiral of low expectations; therefore, you don't make the effort necessary to go above and beyond what you've done in the past.

Chapter Five

Prepare for the Battle!

Therefore take up the whole armor of God, that you may be able to withstand in the evil day and having done all, to stand. Stand therefore, having girded your waist with truth, having put on the breastplate of righteousness, and having shod your feet with the preparation of the gospel of peace; above all, taking the SHIELD OF FAITH with which you will be able to quench all the fiery darts of the wicked one. And the helmet of salvation, and SWORD OF THE SPIRIT, which is the WORD of God:

(Ephesians 6: 13-17)

"The probability that we may fall in the struggle ought not to deter us from the support of a cause we believe to be just."

Abraham Lincoln

Whether you prevail against your Giant or not will ultimately be determined by your preparation for the battle. Proper preparation is crucial. David understood this fact even as a young man. Though later in his life he became an outstanding tactical and strategic fighter, this fight against the giant Goliath was neither tactical nor strategic for him. It was won on his sheer FAITH and TRUST in God, as well as his reliance on his proven human abilities!

Use Your Own Weapons of Warfare

Neither Saul nor any of the fighting men of Israel understood how to fight this giant Goliath. When David told Saul that he would fight the giant, Saul offered him HIS armor:

And Saul said to David, "Go, and the Lord be with you!" So Saul clothed David with his armor, and he put a bronze helmet on his head; he also clothed him with a coat of mail. David fastened his sword to his armor and tried to walk, for he had not tested them. And David said to Saul, "I cannot walk with these, for I have not tested them." So David took them off.

(1 Samuel 17: 37-39)

Unfortunately, all Saul could offer David were the weapons of warfare that he used for fighting. David tried on Saul's fighting gear and it didn't fit him. This is one of the most important aspects of preparing for spiritual warfare that you need to understand and follow, because it could explain why you have failed to defeat your Giants in the past and why they will continue to wreak havoc and cause ridicule in your life. When David fastened Saul's sword to the armor, he couldn't even walk much less fight a giant in it! He said; 'Thanks but no thanks, besides, I haven't even tested them!' ***"Armor"*** in this case means-advice. When you are faced with a problem, situation or circumstance, there are people in your life who have a tendency to try and impose their armor (advice) on you about how you should deal with it. Be careful whose armor you use to attack your Giants! David was not foolish enough to go into battle against a foe that could kill him using someone else's untested and unsuccessful methods.

How often have you used someone else's untested armor, advice or methods to attack your Giants and were successful? Very seldom, I'm sure. When you tried to use their armor to fight your Giant, you probably got defeated every time. Unfortunately these tend to be people who are closest to you, like family members, best friends, co-workers, sometimes even pastors and ministers. You feel pressured because you don't want to hurt their feelings by not taking their armor, so you take it, and many times get crushed in the battle against your Giant. They have good intentions and they mean well, but it still doesn't change the fact that it is their armor that's meant for their fight, not yours. If their armor and battle tactics are not working for them in their fight against their Giants, and usually it isn't, then why would you want to use it against yours? These well meaning but ignorant people, as it relates to spiritual warfare, can only help you be as successful as they have been.

Understand this simple truth: "*Most people can only fight with the level of knowledge and understanding with which they are use to fighting with.*" In other words, '**they can only give you what they have and are familiar with using**!' If the Giants you are facing require a different mindset or knowledge than they possess, would it be wise for you to accept their advice for your situation or circumstance? Regardless of how well intentioned their advice is, it simply won't work for you. However, if you still want to consider using their armor because of who they are in your life, I suggest you qualify it by asking yourself two questions:

FIRST: Are they prevailing against the Giants in their own life using their armor?

SECOND: Would I want the results they are getting if I used their armor?

If your answer is yes to both questions and it fits your situation, then by all means, use it. If not, then do like David did with Saul's armor; respectfully drop their armor at their feet like David, and decline their offer. Also, if you have been using the same conventional methods to fight your Giants and they haven't been working, let me explain why that might be. First of all, Saul and the men of Israel had been fighting the Philistines for years. They would win a battle here and there and lose a battle here and there, but they never totally defeated them. Why? The reason is because *they were both equally matched with their weapons of warfare.*

Saul and the men of Israel and the Philistines were fighting with the same armor, methods, mentality...etc. Note the description of Goliath's armor:

He had a bronze helmet on his head, and he was armed with a coat of mail, and the weight of the coat was five thousand shekels of bronze. And he had bronze armor on his legs and a bronze javelin between his shoulders. Now the staff of his spear was like a weaver's beam, and his iron spearhead weighed six hundred shekels:

(*1 Samuel 17: 5-7*)

No doubt impressive. But look at what Saul offered David to go into battle with Goliath using:

So Saul clothed David with his armor, and he put a BRONZE HELMET on his head; he also clothed him with a COAT of MAIL.

(*1 Samuel 38*)

Sound familiar? The same armor (weapons) cancelling out the other's effectiveness. This is why your battle seems to go on and on, back and forth, and you never completely get the victory over your Giants. The same force, energy, mentality, emotions and limited financial resources that you are using to fight your Giants, are being used against you in a *counter attack*, therefore you will never be able to prevail against them. This kind of back and forth keeps you on the defensive and you will continue to be unsuccessful until you change your tactics. You may win a battle or a skirmish here or there, but winning a battle or skirmish here or there only means that every now and then you get a break from the Giant's attack; maybe on the weekend the bill collectors won't call, or you won't see the person you fear for a while, perhaps you can take the phone off of the hook or something happens that gives you some relief, but just like clockwork, the Giant rears its ugly head again at the appointed time, like at the first or the end of the month when the bills come due, the next company meeting when you will see that person again, or when the abuser gets home or after they've had another drink....etc. You see what I mean? This can go on for years. You never really kill and defeat it; you just numb yourself from its attacks until the next time.

Arm Yourself

Rather than just go tit-for-tat with Goliath like Saul and the men of Israel had done in the past, David *took the fight to another level!* And so must you! David armed himself with proven weapons that he knew would work:

> *Then he took his STAFF in his hand; and he chose for himself FIVE SMOOTH STONES from the brook, and put them in the shepherd's bag, in a pouch which he had, and his sling was in his hand.*
>
> *(1 Samuel 17: 40)*

David armed himself with:

    A. His STAFF
    B. Five SMOOTH stones
    C. His SLING

Let's look at the significance of why these weapons were chosen in particular and what they represented.

The Staff:

The shepherd's staff is commonly used by shepherds to guide the sheep and to ward off enemies of the sheep. David had used his shepherd's staff as a weapon before, and was very familiar and comfortable using it. He felt that it would serve him in battle if necessary; in fact he used it to kill a lion that attacked the sheep:

> *But David said to Saul, "Your servant used to keep his father's sheep, and when a lion or a bear came near and took a lamb out of the flock, I went out after it and struck it, and delivered the lamb from its mouth; and when it arose against me, I caught it by its beard, and struck and killed it..."*
>
> *(1 Samuel 17: 34-35)*

Notice David said he 'went out and struck it (this was with the rock in the sling which could be used at a distance) and delivered the lamb, BUT when the lion rose up against me, I caught its beard, and struck it-with the staff (used for close quarter combat) and killed it.' David was prepared for any contingency. If the rock didn't work on the lion, he knew he had the staff, which he was experienced using as well. When David went after Goliath, he had his staff and rocks, because he wanted to be prepared for any contingency. If one didn't work, he knew the other would. Why is this significant? It's significant because David knew he was going to kill the giant, that wasn't his concern; he just wanted OPTIONS as far as how he would do it! Which method would get the job done didn't matter, the stick or the stone, he could use either. Five stones and one staff, SIX options, Goliath didn't stand a chance!

Are you prepared for contingencies as you launch your attack on your Giants? I've often heard "church people" say; "Faith doesn't need a backup plan," well I beg to differ. If you had the kind of faith that moved mountains, which you can develop, perhaps you don't need a backup plan; however most people don't have that kind of faith, *yet*, so I suggest you give yourself as many options for victory as possible. If you knew you had six options or methods of attacking and defeating your Giants and that God could use any one of them to give you the victory, how confident would you be in launching YOUR attack? David was ready for an "aerial" assault or "hand-to-hand" combat if necessary, it didn't matter. He was prepared. Goliath was unaware of the campaign that was about to be launched against him! Maybe the reason your Giants can intimidate you the way that they do is because you are only seeing ONE way of defeating them, and if you shoot your best shot and it doesn't work, you would be *out of options*. Therefore, you are so paralyzed by the fear of confronting them with your "One option" tactic, that you're not sure will work in the first place, that you do nothing.

Snap out of it! Expand your options and increase your chances for victory! Take the time now to list a minimum of four ways you can launch an attack on your Giants TODAY! What CAN you do TODAY? Don't limit your thinking like you have in the past. There may be more than four, but get something down on paper that you can do now. It doesn't matter how unreasonable it may seem at the moment, get started, write something! You have to go on the offensive and attack your Giants! You can't continue to play defense and expect to win against this enemy. You have been playing defense all this time and where has it gotten you? Go after them with whatever God gives you, even if it's stones!

The 5 Smooth Stones:

Next, David took five "smooth" stones from the brook. What was the significance of the smooth stones? David chose smooth stones because they could SAIL WITHOUT DRAG! The aerodynamics of the smooth stones was different from "jagged" edged ones. A jagged stone causes too much drag which causes them not to sail, as fast, as far or be as accurate as smooth stones. Metaphorically speaking; doubt, fear, hesitation, bitterness, anger, selfishness, disbelief, mistrust, envy, jealousy, uncertainty and lack of faith represent the "drag" that causes a decrease in velocity and the inaccuracy of "jagged" edged stones, and will hinder any effort you make to defeat your Giants. This emotional, physical, mental, financial, and psychological drag causes you to deliberate, procrastinate and drawback, therefore your effectiveness will be compromised and you will fail to make the maximum impact against your Giants. Are you using smooth or jagged edged stones in your attack against your Giants?

David did not want anything to slow his stones down before they reached their intended target, Goliath. He knew God could not use the jagged stones of doubt, fear, bitterness, jealousy, or any other distraction to achieve the objective, which was VICTORY over the giant! David's perspective was that he didn't see an invincible giant; he saw an opportunity to bring honor and glory to his God with this victory.

The First Stone-*SPEECH*

> *"For out of the abundance of the heart the mouth speaks. For by your words you will be justified, and by your words you will be condemned."*
>
> *(Matthew 12: 34, 37)*

It's no wonder the first stone David put into his pouch was the stone of ***speech***. He recognized the fact that whatever came from his mouth God was going to use against the giant. He knew that he would speak either *victory* or *defeat* into his encounter with Goliath, the choice was his:

> *Then David SAID to the Philistine, "You come to me with a sword, with a spear, and with a javelin, BUT I come to you in the name of the Lord of hosts, the God of the armies of Israel, whom YOU have defied, This day the Lord will deliver YOU into MY hand, and I will strike you and take your head from you."*
>
> *(1 Samuel 17: 45-46)*

David applied the universal law of *Profession,* ***"exomologeo"*** {ex-om-ol-og-eh'-o}, which in Greek means to confess, to profess, and acknowledge openly and joyfully, to one's honor, to profess that one would do something they promised. Being careful to watch what you profess out of your mouth is critical to your success in your battle. Your words will create victory or defeat in your life. The children of Israel found this out early in their journey out of Egypt, and as a result, spent forty years wandering in the desert unnecessarily because of what they "spoke" into their lives. Most people have heard the story of how the children of Israel wandered in the desert for forty years, but the story often puzzled me. I never really understood why it took them forty years to make what was essentially a two week journey-from Egypt to Canaan (the Promised Land). Why were they in the desert for so long; was God punishing them; did they not know the way; what was the purpose of taking so long to do something that should have been done in a short period of time? I didn't realize until after I really read the account of the story that God was simply *giving them what they* *"professed!"*

After God miraculously delivered the children of Israel out of Pharaoh's bondage in Egypt, before they entered the Promised Land, He told Moses to have each family choose a representative to go and survey the land:

> *And the Lord spoke to Moses, saying, "Send men to spy out the* *land of Canaan, which I am giving to the children of Israel;* *from each tribe of their fathers you shall send a man, every* *one a leader among them."*
>
> *(Numbers 13:1-2)*

Each family (tribe) chose a leader from among it to go and "spy out the land" for forty days and bring back an assessment of whether the land was good and plentiful for them to occupy. When each family representative returned with their assessment, all but two of them brought back a report that was less favorable:

> *And they returned from spying out the land after forty days.* *They departed and came back to Moses and all the* *congregation of the children of Israel; they brought back word* *to them and to all the congregation, and showed them the* *fruit of the land. Then they told him, and said: "We went to the* *land where you sent us. It truly flows with milk and honey,* ***Nevertheless,*** *the people who dwell in the land are strong; the* *cities are fortified, we are not able to go up against the people* *for they are stronger than we, and we are like grasshoppers in* *our own sight, and so we were in their sight."*
>
> *(Numbers 13: 25, 26-28, 31, 35)*

When the people feared the report delivered by the spies of the land, they spoke against Moses and Aaron:

> *So all the congregation lifted up their voice and cried, and the* *people wept that night. And all the children of Israel* *complained against Moses and Aaron, and the whole* *congregation said to them, "If only we had died in the land of* *Egypt! Or if only we had died in this wilderness! Why has the*

Lord brought us to this land to fall by the sword, that our
wives and children should become victims?"

(Numbers 14: 1-3)

This is it! This is where you really have to be careful what comes out of your mouth as it relates to God and attacking your Giants! God's response explains why **what you speak is what you get:**

And the Lord spoke to Moses and Aaron, saying, "How long
shall I bear with this evil congregation who complain against
Me? I have heard the complaints which the children of Israel
make against Me. Say to them, 'As I live,' say's the Lord, 'just
as you have **spoken** *in My hearing,* **so will I do to you:** *The*
carcasses of you who complained against me shall fall in this
wilderness, all of you who were numbered from twenty years
and above. You shall by no means enter the land which I swore
I will make you dwell in. But your little ones, whom you said
would be victims, I will bring in, and they shall know the land
which you have despised. You sons shall be shepherds in the
wilderness forty years, according to the number of the days in
which you spied out the land, forty days, for each day you shall
bear your guilt one year, namely **forty years...**"

(Numbers 14: 26-31, 33-34)

Yes, to God, it's that serious! They professed it and He manifested it!

This law of Profession is just as real and true as the law of gravity. It is a universal law of God; He 'SPOKE' creation into existence:

In the beginning God created the heavens and the earth. The
earth was without form, and void; and the darkness was on the
face of the deep. Then God SAID, "Let there be light"; and there
was light.

(Genesis 1: 1, 3)

Then God SAID, "Let there be a firmament in the midst of the
waters, and let it divide the waters from the waters."

(Genesis 1: 6)

God spoke and it was done! From Genesis 1: verse 1 to verse 31 we see God speaking the entire universe into being, the Earth, the heavens, water divisions, land divisions, plants and vegetation, fish and fowl, even MAN was SPOKEN into existence!

David's professions were:

> *I trust in You O Lord; I say, "You are my God." My times are in Your hand; Deliver me from the hand of my enemies, and from those who persecute me.*
>
> *(Psalm 31: 14-15)*

> *Delight yourself in the Lord, And He shall give you the desires of your heart. Commit your way to the Lord, trust also in Him and He shall bring it to pass.*
>
> *(Psalm 37: 4-5)*

Do not play with this or take this law lightly thinking God knows what you mean. Remember, God is SPECIFIC! The Holy Spirit will bring to you whatever you are professing out of your mouth; good or bad, it does not discern one from the other. Make sure what you are saying is what you want...because you will get it.

David also applied the universal law of *Confession;* **"*homologeo*"** { hom-ol-og-eh'-o}, which in Greek means 'to say what has been said, saying the same thing as another, i.e. to agree with.' David knew that if God said something, or made a promise, then He would fulfill it, because HE COULD NOT LIE! Promises and Covenants were God's Word. He would NEVER go against His Word:

> *"I will declare and decree: The Lord has SAID to Me, You are My son, Today I begotten You. Ask of Me and I will give You The nations for Your inheritance, And the ends of the earth for Your possession. You shall break them with a rod of iron; You shall dash them to pieces like a potter's vessel."*
>
> *(Psalm: 2: 7-9)*

> *"Surely blessings I will bless you, and multiplying I will multiply you."*
>
> *(Hebrews: 6: 14)*

"Who has put wisdom in the mind? Or who has given understanding to the heart?"

(Job 38: 36)

"No weapon formed against you shall prosper, and every tongue which rises against you in judgment You shall condemn. This is the heritage of the servants of the Lord, and their righteousness is from Me." Says the Lord.

(Isaiah 56: 17)

David simply repeated what God said about him receiving the victory, and confirmed it by the words of his mouth. Since David wrote the Psalms, you can read many of the professions and confessions he made to God which allowed him to be victorious over his enemies, Goliath included. What are you unknowingly confessing and professing out of your mouth and into your life? Are you speaking blessings, triumph, success, favor and protection into your life or are you speaking failure, loss, defeat, lack, strife and curses into it? You hold the key with your words. The Holy Spirit will honor what you say! Remember these assumingly harmless comments; 'if it ain't one thing it's. . .' 'If it wasn't for bad luck I'd have no . . .,' 'I can't win for. . .,' or statements like, 'nobody loves me,' 'this won't work,' 'I can't find a job,' 'nobody's hiring,' 'times are tough'. . .etc.

You are speaking these things into your life every time you make those comments. Guard your tongue and therefore your words:

The tongue is so set among our members that it defiles the whole body, and sets on fire the course of nature; and it is set on fire by hell.

(James 3: 6)

But no man can tame the tongue. It is an unruly evil, full of deadly poison. With it we bless our God and Father, and with it we curse men, who have been made in the similitude of God. Out of the same mouth proceed blessings and cursing.

(James 3: 8-10)

As you can see, taming the tongue may not be easy, but it is certainly necessary in order to defeat your Giants. What are you saying to your Giants? Are you speaking victory or defeat, abundance or lack, blessings or curses? Are you giving the Giant power over you with your tongue or are you taking your power back?

Here is what God has promised you. This is what you can stand on, confess and decree. Jesus said:

> *If you ask ANYTHING in My name, I WILL DO IT.*
>
> *(John 14: 14)*

> *"Ask, and it WILL be given to you; seek, and you WILL find; knock, and it WILL be opened to you. For EVERYONE who asks receives, and he who seeks finds, and to him who knocks IT WILL be opened."*
>
> *(Matthew 7: 7-8)*

> *'For assuredly, I say to you, if you have faith as a mustard seed, you WILL say to this mountain, 'Move from here to there, and IT WILL MOVE: and NOTHING will be impossible for you.'*
>
> *(Matthew 17: 20)*

> *"With men it is impossible, BUT not with God; for with God ALL THINGS ARE POSSIBLE."*
>
> *(Mark 10: 27)*

These are just a few of God's promises. You can search the Bible for several other scriptures in which to arm yourself. He will confirm to you like He did with David, that He has given you the ability to have victory over any Giant that you face. Don't doubt it; DO IT! Start professing and confessing victory over your Giants. Your words are your armor for success as God promised.

The Second Stone – *FAITH*

> *I will bless the Lord who has given me counsel; My heart also instructs me in the night seasons. I have set the Lord always before me; Because He is at my right hand I shall not be moved.*
>
> *(Psalm 16: 7-8)*

David put the stone of **faith** into his pouch. He was prepared to sling it next because of his faith in God to deliver the result. After David had gathered the stones, HE went after Goliath. His FAITH took him there:

> *And he drew near the Philistine. So the Philistine came, and began drawing near David.*
>
> *(1 Samuel: 40-41)*

David drew near Goliath first, and then Goliath began drawing near David. Goliath didn't seem too eager to engage David in battle. Your Giants won't be either when they see that you aren't running away like you did in the past. They will move timidly towards you, because they sense something is different this time. When your enemies see that you aren't backing down, they aren't as bold to confront you as they once were. When you stand up to your Giants and decide that "this is it, I will not back down," you will see a change in their attitude, but more importantly, you will see a change in YOURS. You will develop a resolve to take a stand like never before. Whatever happens, you are there for the duration; you are going to see this through. You are taking a stand and saying; "Giant, you can either fight or flee, it doesn't matter, but I'm not going anywhere!"

As David's true motive surfaced the encounter grew intense:

> *"And this day I will give the carcasses of the camp of the Philistines to the birds of the air and the wild beasts of the earth, that all the earth may know that there is a God in Israel. Then all this assembly shall know that the Lord does not save with sword and spear; for THE BATTLE IS THE LORD'S and HE will give you into our hands."*
>
> *(1 Samuel 17: 46-47)*

David said to Goliath in essence; 'enough with the talking, let's get on with it, I am going to defeat you and cut your head off and then I am going to give your carcass, and that of ALL the Philistines to the birds of the air and the wild beast of the earth!' David had faith that God would fight his battle and give him the victory! He knew that Goliath and the Philistines did not honor or acknowledge the Lord his God. He wanted them to do so; but more importantly, he wanted the children of Israel to stop trusting in their own ability to defeat the enemy with their swords and spears, and realize that the Philistines had no covenant with God, and they did, and the Lord their God would fight for them again if they would just put their trust in Him. Your victory against your Giants will not come by the might of your hands with swords and spears either.

God has a covenant with you too, and He will honor it. As you adopt David's perspective and attitude to attack your Giants, you will learn to fight with the same weaponry he used:

> *Therefore take up the whole armor of God, that you may be able to withstand in the evil day and having done all, to stand. Stand therefore, having girded your waist with truth, having put on the breastplate of righteousness, and having shod your feet with the preparation of the gospel of peace; above all, taking the SHIELD OF FAITH with which you will be able to quench all the fiery darts of the wicked one. And the helmet of salvation, and SWORD OF THE SPIRIT, which is the WORD of God:*
>
> *(Ephesians 6: 13-17)*

Two of the most powerful weapons David used against Goliath were the 'Shield of FAITH' and the 'SWORD of the Spirit' which is the "Word" of God! Faith in the word of God is crucial to your victory.

The Third Stone-*HOPE*

> *For You are my hope, O Lord GOD; You are my trust from my youth. By You I have been upheld from birth You are He who took me out of my mother's womb. My praise shall be continually of You.*
>
> *(Psalm 71: 5-6)*

David's third stone represented the *hope* he had for the future of his nation. He saw that they were bound by fear of the Philistines and were more focused on them than they were on the power and ability of their God to fight for them. He felt the only way they would reach their full potential as a nation was to have this reproach of fear removed from them so that they could return to trusting God. He was fighting for his family's survival! Usually you will fight more fiercely for others than you would for yourself, especially when it comes to anything that threatens the health, welfare and peace of mind of your wife, husband, child, parents, grandparents and so forth. When David saw how afraid his family was of Goliath, he knew he had to do something. He was not going to stand around and allow this giant to continue interfering with the blessings his family should be enjoying, if it were not for them focusing so much of their attention on the fear of him:

> *And all the men of Israel, when they saw the man (Goliath), fled from him and were dreadfully afraid. So the men of Israel said, 'Have you seen this man who has come up? Surely he has come up to defy Israel...'*
>
> *(1 Samuel 17: 25)*

The fear of Goliath had the men and the nation of Israel mentally, emotionally and psychologically paralyzed, much like the effects the current financial upheaval and state of the economy is having on families today. Record layoffs, unemployment, job losses, bank failures, frozen credit, foreclosures, repossessions, bankruptcies, corporate greed...etc, all play a part in creating a sense of uncertainty for the future. Like David, you may be carrying the weight of restoring hope to your family, business and community in your heart. Success can seem like a daunting and distant reality, but if you, put the situation in its proper perspective, you can achieve the results he did. You serve the same God. When you apply the same principles and mindset that David did, you can attack your Giants with confidence and the assurance of victory.

God's Promise is certain. Regardless of what the situation looks like, have your HOPE and security grounded in God's Word:

When God made His promise to Abraham, since there was no one greater for Him to swear by, He swore by Himself, saying, "I will surely bless you and give you many descendants." And so after waiting patiently, Abraham received what was promised.

(Hebrews 6: 13-14 NIV)

Because God wanted to make the unchanging nature of his purpose very clear to the heirs of what was promised, he confirmed it with an oath. God did this so that, by two unchangeable things in which it is impossible for God to lie, we who have fled to take hold of the hope offered to us may be greatly encouraged. We have this hope as an anchor for the soul, firm and secure.

(Hebrews 6: 13-19 NIV)

When God promised Abraham that he was going to bless him and his wife Sarah with many descendants, they didn't even have a child between the two of them, and besides that, Abraham was ninety-nine years old and his wife Sarah was eighty-nine. Yet it didn't matter how "impossible" it may have looked for them to conceive a child at that age, they kept their hope in God's word and Abraham didn't falter in his belief that God would deliver on what He promised. Because it is so important to God that He keeps His promises and oaths, He swore upon Himself, because there was no one greater. You and I are the result of God having kept that promise to Abraham, and He is still keeping that promise, even today. We are Abraham's descendents and heirs!

Therefore it is of faith that it might be according to grace, so that the promise might be sure to all the seed, those who are of the faith of Abraham, who is the father of us all. God, who gives life to the dead and calls those things which do not exist as though they did; who contrary to HOPE, in the HOPE believed, so that he became the father of many nations.

(Romans 4: 16-18)

If you keep the same hope that David and Abraham had, and do not waver in your desire for a brighter future and outlook for you, your family or business, things will begin working in your favor.

Knowing and believing that God will deliver on what He promises, enables you to defeat your Giants, no matter how big, ferocious, impossible or intimidating they may appear right now. Remember, God 'calls those things that do not exist as though they did,' because He is the One who ultimately determines the outcome according to His purpose and desire for your life, not your Giant. God will always have the last word in every situation. Even if you don't see how it will work out, just know that it will:

> *Therefore my heart is glad, and my glory rejoices; My flesh also will rest in HOPE.*
>
> *(Psalm 16: 9)*

The Fourth Stone-*BELIEF*

> *For by You I can run against a troop, By my God I can leap over a wall. As for God, His way is PERFECT; The word of the Lord is PROVEN; He is a shield to all who trust Him. For who is God, except the Lord? And who is a rock, except our God? It is God who arms me with strength, And makes my way perfect.*
>
> *(Psalm 18: 29-32)*

David dropped the stone of *belief* into his pouch next. He had complete and unwavering belief that God was going to protect him in the battle with Goliath and that He would keep him safe. He knew God was the source of everything he had ever accomplished, or ever would accomplish in his life, and this was just the beginning of a long and loving relationship. He knew that he wouldn't be defeated at the hands of this giant. His belief in the Lord and His promise of protection was so strong; it gave him the courage to ATTACK HIS GIANT!

When you decide to take a stand against your Giants, be prepared for them to rise up and fight back, especially in the beginning. This is not the time or the place for you to back down, be fearful and doubt. Your Giant has controlled your life for a while. It has become used to the grip it has held on you. When you set out to release yourself from its grip, the battle will seem more intense, more fierce and harder to overcome; your anxiety will tempt you to quit. Feelings you never knew you had before will rise up and begin to play tricks on your mind. This is the point in the battle where prayer, fasting, Bible study and believing are essential. When you begin to confront this Giant; your old self, old habits, old attitudes and old desires will want to step in and make you do what you've done in the past which is give in or give up! But not this time; you will have to fight the urge to quit, lie down or surrender. Anxiety, temptation, resistance to change, fear, insecurity, uncertainty, depression, and all of the old feelings you've had before when you've taken a stand will come upon you, but you must resist them and keep moving toward the Giant.

One way you can keep going is to repeat your favorite scriptures, chant them if necessary, but don't give in to the temptation to quit. Had David gotten scared and run when he saw Goliath coming toward him, everything he had hoped for, prayed for, sacrificed for, spoken of and dreamed about would have been lost, and so it will be with you. It's all on the line. For the sake of your family, career, business or community, stand and fight! Believe that you can overcome the fear, anxiety, procrastination and temptation by focusing on the *prize*, not the process. Remember why you attacked this Giant in the first place! Focus on what you hoped to gain, like your; emotional freedom, piece of mind, release from worry or to win your wife, husband or children back, security for your family, confidence or self respect! It is said that anything worth having is worth fighting for. I think you will agree!

David was clear about his reasons. His reasons empowered him and so should YOURS! He believed that defeating Goliath would accomplish three things that he felt very strongly about and to which he was committed.

He wanted to:

1. ***GLORIFY GOD*** He wanted God to get the "Glory from the story!"

"I come to you in the name of the Lord of the hosts, the God of the armies of Israel, whom you have defied. This day THE LORD will deliver you into my hand."
(1 Samuel 45-46)

David wanted the people of the land to know that God delivered the victory. How dare Goliath or anyone else defy the Lord God of Israel!

2. ***BENEFIT HIS PEOPLE*** This was a threefold benefit:

   A. He would remove the fear Goliath had over the people of Israel:

And all the men of Israel, when they saw the man, fled from him and were dreadfully afraid.
(1 Samuel 17: 24)

   B. He would remove the reproach he felt God had on them, because they had rejected God's divine theocratic leadership. After the death of Joshua, God made Samuel a judge over Israel, yet God divinely led them himself. When Samuel had grown old, Israel asked for a king (a man) to rule over them like they saw the other nations had, so God took his hand off of the nation because of their disobedience. David wanted to restore God's favor upon them:

Then the elders of Israel gathered together and came to Samuel as Ramah, and said to him, "Look, you are old, and your sons do not walk in your ways. Now make us a king to judge us like all the nations." But the thing displeased Samuel when they said, "Give us a king to judge us." So Samuel prayed to the Lord, And the Lord said to Samuel, "Heed the voice of the people in all that they say to you; for they have not rejected you, but they have rejected Me, that I should not reign over them. According to all the works that they have done since the day that I brought them up out of Egypt, even to this day-with which they have forsaken Me and served other gods-so they are doing to you also. Now therefore, heed their voice. HOWEVER, you shall solemnly forewarn them, and show them the behavior of the king who will reign over them."

(1 Samuel 8: 4-9)

    C. That the people will trust in God to fight for them and not in their own abilities;

"Then all THIS assembly shall know that the Lord does not save with sword and spear; for the battle is the Lord's and He will give you into our hands."

(1 Samuel 17: 47)

3. **CHANGE**- He would be different as a result of defeating the giant.

David felt that when God delivered him from the hand of the giant, his faith and trust in God to protect him would go to another level. God had anointed him to be the next king of Israel, and he knew that he would have to have a faith in God that would see him through any challenge he would face as the leader of the nation, and he wanted the people to follow him.

It has been said that if your WHY is strong and compelling enough and you are committed to it, then the *how* would be irrelevant. You will simply do what is necessary to get the job done. David's focus wasn't on the giant; it was on the JOY... the joy that would come from God getting the glory for this great victory and the redemption of his people. The joy of seeing his people delivered from the fear of Goliath and having God's favor restored upon them once again. The "PRIZE" of success was more important than the "PROCESS" necessary to achieve it. How about you? What are your compelling reasons for "Attacking Your Giants?" Are you passionate, committed, determined, focused, fired up and excited about defeating your Giants and removing the scourge they are having over your life, family, joy, peace, happiness, career, business? You should be! Get after them! Trust God to deliver the result!

The FIFTH Stone- *TRUST*

> *O, Lord my God, in You I put my trust; Save me from all those who persecute me; And deliver me, Lest they tear me like a lion, Rending me in pieces, while there is none to deliver.*
>
> *(Psalm 7: 1-2)*

Then David put the stone of ***trust*** into his pouch. He trusted that God would see him through to victory. He didn't know exactly how God would do it nor did it matter; he simply trusted that He would. The people had already decided Goliath was too much of a terror for them to fight. They trusted in their abilities to fight the Philistines and had not been very successful in defeating them up to that point, so no one wanted to go out and do battle with this giant. If David had not dealt with him, the nation of Israel would have just tolerated him terrorizing them indefinitely. Isn't that a sad way to live, miserably tolerating something or someone in your life because you don't think you can do anything about it or you don't have the courage to address it? You need to rid yourself of this kind of thinking now. David knew he couldn't count on anyone except God to help him. Not that it mattered, but perhaps he would have liked to have had some of his fellow countrymen to stand with him to defeat this giant to show unity in the nation. Sometimes we would like help conquering our Giants; however be cautious when soliciting the help of others. There are some people who will help you to achieve something, and then as a result of their help, they think you owe them and they seldom let you forget it.

Sometimes getting help from others can hurt you in the long run, because with their help you may achieve results, but it may not be what God intended for you. Now you've missed a great opportunity to exercise your faith and trust in Him to see you through defeating this or other Giants that will eventually arise in your life later. You will always be looking for help from someone or something other than God in the future. Remember, they may not be there for you the next time, but God will, He never fails. Learning to truly trust Him totally may not be easy in the beginning, but He is the best weapon you have to attack and defeat your Giants for good.

> *Trust in the Lord with all your heart, And lean not on your own understanding; In all your ways acknowledge Him, And He shall direct your paths.*
> *(Proverbs 3: 5)*

The Sling: *ACTION*

> *What good is it, my brothers, if a man claims to have faith but has no deeds? Can such faith save him? Suppose a brother or sister is without clothes and daily food. If one of you says to him, "Go, I wish you well; keep warm and well fed," but does nothing about his physical needs, what good is it? In the same way, faith by itself, if it is not accompanied by ACTION, IS DEAD.*
> *(James 2: 14-17 NIV)*

The sling represents *ACTION!* Action is the most powerful weapon you can have in your arsenal. Action puts the power of all the stones into effect. Without it, nothing works. **God won't move until you do!** When you pray, fast, confront or reach out to them, you are taking action steps to begin dealing with the fear of your Giants, and face them head on with confidence. This totally disorients them. They don't know what to expect, because you've never done this before. This is **"out of character"** for you. Unfortunately, this is where most people fail to maximize the power of the stones. They fail to take the actions necessary to defeat their Giants. You can speak to your Giant, have trust, have hope, believe and have faith, but if you don't take any actions against them, none of that matters. It's just a "dream deferred." Until you take action and do like David did, "draw near to the Philistine," you will be in the same place and the same situation this time next year and perhaps the year after that. Action is critical to success in warfare.

David TOOK ACTION towards defeating Goliath. He didn't sit around and think about it, talk about it, contemplate, deliberate or hypothecate about the giant. He got up and DID SOMETHING! David acted out of character from what most of the men who faced Goliath had done in the past. **He took the fight to Goliath!** This threw Goliath off because other men he fought usually were so intimidated by him that they fled before the battle began, but not David. Not only did David confront him, but he took the one action that made all the difference in the outcome of the battle.

What was the action that David took you might ask? Simple...He **"Threw The Rock!"** That's it...he threw the Rock. He did what was within HIS power and ability to do! Many times, the action it takes to conquer and defeat the Giants in your life is something simple. I didn't say it is always easy, but usually it's simple. The problem is you have tied so much emotion, hurt and fear into taking action that you are afraid to even acknowledge your Giants, much less attack them. You give them the psychological control and advantage over you and the situation; therefore, they control your ability to act. Many times something as simple as making a phone call, offering an apology, letting go of the hurt feelings, forgiving someone, loving someone, understanding someone's concern or trying to see their point of view, can make all the difference in the situation. These actions most of the time require you to set aside your pride and address the issue directly. The conflict, strife, bitterness, negative feelings and emotions, longing or loneliness you suffer as a result of being prideful is real, but these can usually be addressed and resolved relatively easily.

Sometimes the Giants you face are like the one David faced; they are physically intimidating, boisterous and mentally paralyzing. They threaten your financial, physical, emotional and psychological well being. The actions required to defeat them will require a different approach, because they have the potential to cause lasting damage in your life. They have a stronghold on you or your family, business or community's well being, piece of mind and security for far too long, and you are tired of the mental strain they're causing. The results from the actions required to resolve them may take a while to manifest, and will not happen overnight, but don't give up. To change your mindset, attitude and focus takes time. Be patient and encourage yourself as you make the effort.

David didn't always have the mindset he had when he met Goliath. It took time for him to develop it. It took time for him to get to know who God was, how to trust him, or that he could trust him for that matter. It takes time, so don't get discouraged if it doesn't happen overnight. David erred along the way, but he repented and kept working on his relationship with God to become a great king. Take action, pray, fast, read God's word, develop trust and faith in Him, have regular conversations with him like David did. Start now.

Faith without works is dead, so slings (action) are necessary to get results. Some might say that the action David took using the sling to throw the stone that struck Goliath is what did it. Not necessarily. While the sling (action) certainly helped, it wasn't enough to kill the giant. Taking actions towards conquering and defeating your Giant will certainly help in your quest to rid yourself of it, but it takes a little more than that. David could have just thrown the stones with his bare hands (by his thinking about it, praying about it, and fasting about it), while it was a start, it would have had a limited effect. He used the sling (action) to speed up the force and velocity of the stone! Although the sling certainly helped, it still would not have generated enough speed and force to exact the kind of damage that it would take to topple Goliath. What was it that he did that made the difference?

Remember, Goliath wore a bronze helmet in battle. The stone would have had to sail through the air with enough force and at such high velocity, that it could penetrate the bronze helmet and sink into his forehead. David was just a boy. He didn't have the physical strength to throw a stone that hard, plus he was running towards Goliath when he threw it, so his feet were not planted firmly, which could have taken some of the zip off of the stone. How did the stone gather that much force and velocity to cause it to penetrate the helmet and into Goliath's forehead? David just "slung" the stone.

> *So it was, when the Philistine arose and came and drew near to meet David, that David HURRIED AND RAN TOWARD the army to meet the Philistine. Then David put his hand in his bag and took out a stone; and he SLUNG IT and struck the Philistine in his forehead, so that the stone sank into his forehead, and he fell on his face to the earth.*
>
> *(1 Samuel 17: 48-49)*

The reason is the power wasn't in David slinging the stone; the POWER was in him slinging the stone combined with his WORDS, his HOPE, his TRUST, his BELIEF, along with his FAITH, and having it delivered by GOD'S HAND that made the IMPACT on Goliath's forehead that toppled him! Sure, David THREW it, but God **DELIVERED** it!

That's what killed the giant! He was hit with the power of ALL FIVE stones delivered by the **HAND OF GOD! POW!** One shot! Down went Goliath! David believed God could kill the giant and He did.

That's how you will topple your Giants, not by your power and might, but by God's, along with your hopes, and desires to be victorious. Don't fear your Giants; take action against them! Attack them NOW! God has assured you the victory. Trust Him to fight for you like He did David. David did what he could do about the situation and left the results to God. How about you? Will you do what you can about your situation, and trust God to deliver the results and accept however it turns out? Use the combined force of your words, faith, hope, belief and trust, and take action-throw the rock-and topple your Giants. Trust God to deliver the results.

And he shall say to them, 'Hear, O Israel: Today you are on the verge of battle with your enemies. Do not let your heart faint, do not be afraid, and do not tremble or be terrified because of them; for the Lord your God is He who goes with you, to fight for you against your enemies, to save you.'

(Deuteronomy 20: 3-4)

Just like God fought for and assured Israel, He fights for and assures you. He commands you not to be afraid or tremble at the sight of your enemies, but stand still and witness His glory. The more you follow David's lead in developing your relationship with God, the more you will begin to see Him act on your behalf and in your favor. Soon you will get to that place in your walk with Him where like David, you....

Chapter Six

Find the SWEET SPOT!

Blessed is the man Who walks not in the counsel of the ungodly, Nor stands in the path of sinners, Nor sits in the seat of the scornful; But his delight is in the law of the Lord, and in His law he meditates day and night. He shall be like a tree planted by the rivers of water, That brings forth its fruit in its season, whose leaf also shall not wither; And WHATEVER HE DOES SHALL PROSPER.

(Psalm 1: 1-3)

"A dream doesn't become a reality through magic; it takes sweat, determination and hard work."

Colin Powell

David found that place with God where nothing bothered, ruffled, phased or surprised him. He had an assurance from the Lord his God that whatever he did would prosper. He found the "sweet spot!" Some may refer to it as "the zone." You get to a place in your relationship with God where 'you just know that you know' that everything is going to work in your favor because God has shown it to be so for you. This puts you at peace with yourself and others. You really won't be able to explain it. The "sweet spot" comes with earnest prayer, fasting, believing, trust and studying God's word for understanding and clarity. It is a process of discovery that leads to a greater awareness of the power God has placed in you to rise to any occasion and prevail over any Giant in your life. Each victory you experience in God increases your confidence and assurance of knowing that you are not alone; you have a Mighty God who is here to help you attack and kill your Giants:

*So David prevailed over the Philistine with a sling and a stone,
and struck the Philistine and killed him. But there was no
sword in the hand of David. Therefore David ran and stood
over the Philistine, took his sword and drew it out of its sheath
and killed him and cut off his head with it.*

(1 Samuel 17: 50-51)

David was in the "sweet spot" when he attacked Goliath. He
defeated him so fast that afterwards he realized he didn't have a
sword to cut his head off like he said he would. When you defeat the
Giants in your life, don't get so caught up in celebrating your
immediate victory that you don't kill the Giant. Even though you
have defeated it, it may not be "dead" yet. When David realized that
he defeated the giant, but it wasn't "dead" yet, he knew he needed to
finish the task. You might be asking...what's the difference? Defeated
means dead...doesn't it? Not necessarily. You may have won a battle,
and maybe you might get by for a day, a week, or even a month
without reacting to your Giant, or giving in to a person, fear, desire
or temptation, but this is only temporary. Your Giant may not be
dead yet, and it can still rise again.

Recently, I was listening to a popular radio show; the topic was
'people who were in abusive relationships.' There was a woman, who
had called into the show, and she was talking about how her husband
was abusing her and her children. During the call her husband
walked up to her car and was yelling at her and began beating on the
car window for her to open the door or he was going to harm them.
She managed to drive off while still on the phone with the host of the
show. Not knowing where to go, she decided to go to her parent's
house. Throughout the show, the host would call the woman to make
sure she was ok, and asked her to keep him posted on how she was
fairing. Finally, towards the end of the broadcast, she called and
reported that she and the children were safe and had made it to her
parent's home. She said she needed to get the children settled and
would call back later with her progress. She said that she was going
shopping to pick them up some items for the next couple of days

since she left the scene with her husband with only the clothes she and her children had on, but later she would probably have to go back to the house and get the rest of their things for a longer stay.

It was what she said next that floored me and probably most of the other listeners on the call! She asked the host to pray for her that when she goes back to the house to get her and her children's things that she doesn't "DECIDE TO STAY" and try to work things out with the husband! Needless to say, the host was speechless, but he stayed calm about her statement, although he did suggest she didn't contemplate going back for her own safety. Many of the listeners were dumbfounded as well. I'm not sure how it worked out, but this story illustrates what I mean. This lady defeated her Giant, the abusive husband, but she didn't kill it-not her husband-but the emotional and mental ties he had on her. Granted, she wasn't going to immediately forget about the man she was married to for a number of years just like that, but she had to start the process of removing herself and her children from that situation and begin the process of killing the 'hold ties' he had on her and her children, and the fear to which they were constantly subjected.

When you defeat your Giant, to eliminate a future reprisal and attack, you have to kill it by cutting its head off. By cutting off its head, you eliminate its power and influence over you forever. This woman won the immediate battle- she got away from the situation for the moment; however, she didn't kill the Giant, the emotional and psychological stronghold her husband had on her, and she was contemplating returning to that situation. God gave David the victory, but David had to 'kill the giant' himself. Likewise, God will give you the victory, but it is up to you to kill the Giant, and eliminate its present effect and future reprisals in your life. No one else can do this for you.

Then David took Goliath's sword and cut his head off! Why was this important you might be asking? David wanted to assure himself that this giant could never rise up and attack him or the nation of

Israel ever again. That's not to say they would never face Giants in their lives ever again, but it's a fact, they wouldn't be facing **"This"** giant again! Only after you have cut its head off, can you really start to celebrate a victory. Just like David who "removed" the Giant's head from its body, you kill your Giants by removing the people, places, situations, temptations, desires or fears from your life and the debilitating effect they once had on you. When you decide that this is it, this is as far as you go, you have just "drawn the Giant's sword from its sheath!" Slay it once and for all. When you are able to walk away from someone or something knowing that it will not be a factor in your life ever again, you have successfully killed the stronghold, grip, dependence, reliance, and place it held in your life. That is the only way you will know for sure that the Giant is dead in your life, both now and in the future.

When God moves you into the "Sweet Spot"

Then there are times when God will move you into the position of being in the "Sweet Spot" like He did with the children of Israel. When God commanded Moses to bring them out of Egypt, they weren't ready to leave. Even though they were miserable serving Pharaoh, they were more afraid of change and the unknown. There were some who did not want to leave Egypt just because it was all they knew and were familiar with. Like the children of Israel, you may not move on your own either, and therefore, God will move you because He has something greater for you to accomplish. When I was younger and even into my adult years, it was an annual affair in my house to watch The Ten Commandments on television every Easter. Each year when my family and I would watch the movie, one thing I constantly questioned and didn't understand at the time was why did God harden Pharaoh's heart against the children of Israel? When it seemed Pharaoh would soften his stance and was close to letting them leave, the narrator would say; "And God hardened Pharaoh's heart." After that, Pharaoh would get stubborn and not let them go. I never really understood why that was. Then one day, the Holy Spirit led me to read the story and understand the scripture for myself. It seems God was setting Pharaoh up to be instrumental in moving the children of Israel into the "sweet spot." The hardening of Pharaoh's heart by God wasn't against the children of Israel but it was FOR them. It was necessary so that they would not only be free "physically" from Pharaoh's grip, but more importantly it was so they would be free "mentally." When God finally allowed Pharaoh to relent and let the people go, He led them out of Egypt through the wilderness in the direction of the Red Sea. This strategically positioned them to witness the person they feared the most be destroyed once and for all, and to avoid facing their next foe, the Philistines, so soon in their freedom journey:

> Then it came to pass, when Pharaoh had let the people go, that God did not lead them by the way of the land of the Philistines, although that was near; for God said, "Lest they change their minds when they see war, and return to Egypt." So God led the people around by the way of the wilderness of the Red Sea.
> (Exodus 13: 17-18)

God knows His creation! He knew the children of Israel were susceptible to allowing their fear of the unknown make them want go back to the dreadful, albeit familiar situation they had come to know as slaves in Egypt. Many times people would rather stay in circumstances they hate but are familiar with than go through the challenge of changing for something better. In order for God to get you out of your familiar "uncomfort" zone into the "Sweet Spot" He has for you, sometimes He will orchestrate situations and circumstances that will disturb your comfortable position and force you to move. It is all a part of His greater plan and purpose for your life. When it is time for you to move, God will sometimes send a lousy boss, a job, business or financial loss, a bad relationship or marriage, or perhaps even an illness to interrupt your "comfortable" life. This is what happened to the children of Israel. Because God had promised Abraham, Isaac, and Jacob (later named Israel) that after their descendants served for four hundred years in a land that they did not know, and serve a people who would afflict them, then He would bring them out of that land with great riches and bless them and give them a land all their own:

> *Then He (God) said to Abram (later God renamed him Abraham): "Know for a certainty that your descendents will be strangers in a land that is not theirs, and will serve them, and they will afflict them for four hundred years. And also the nation whom they serve I will judge; afterward they shall come out with great possessions."*
>
> *(Genesis 15: 13-14)*

This promise was made to Abram four hundred years earlier. God is a master at timing and keeping promises. He will always keep His word, so it was simply time for the children of Israel to leave Egypt, ready or not, like God said they would. Could it be God may have made a promise to your parents, grandparents or great grandparents about you and He is fulfilling it? It may not seem like it at the moment, but the events that are taking place in your life might be a set up, designed to move you out of where you are to where you should be! The process may not be comfortable to you, but then again these events were not meant for your comfort; they were meant to usher you towards the fulfillment of your destiny. It will be greater later!

The children of Israel had an incredible destiny- to be the "chosen" people of God:

> *And God spoke to Moses and said to him: "I am the Lord. I appeared to Abraham, to Isaac, and to Jacob, as God Almighty, but by My name Lord I was not known to them. I have also established my covenant with them, to give them the land of Canaan, the land of their pilgrimage, in which they were strangers. **I have remembered My covenant.** Therefore say to the children of Israel: 'I am the Lord; I will bring you out from under the burdens of the Egyptians, I will rescue you from their bondage. **I will take you as My people, and I will be your God.** I will bring you into the land which I swore to give to Abraham, Isaac, and Jacob; I will give it to you as a heritage: I am the Lord.' "*
>
> *(Exodus 6: 2-4, 6-8)*

God had to make sure Israel's children didn't blow it by letting the fear of Pharaoh and the unknown paralyze them to the point where they wouldn't move forward, but instead would want to go back to Egypt:

Now the Lord spoke to Moses, saying: "Speak to the children of Israel that they turn and camp before Pi Hahiroth, between Migdol and the sea... For Pharaoh will say of the children of Israel, 'They are bewildered by the land; and the wilderness has closed them in.' Then I will harden Pharaoh's heart, so that he will pursue them; and I will gain honor over Pharaoh and over all his army, that the Egyptians will know that I am Lord."
(Exodus 14: 1-4)

God wanted Pharaoh to pursue the children of Israel. They had to come to a place where in order for them to move into that "Sweet Spot" and live out the promise of their destiny, they had to witness God once and for all remove their greatest fear, Pharaoh, from existence! When Pharaoh realized what he had done by letting the people go from serving Egypt, he pursued them. He went after them with his choice fighting men, chosen chariots, and all of his main army; everyone the children of Israel feared would come after them even if something happened to Pharaoh. When Pharaoh drew near them encamped by the sea, they lifted their eyes and saw the Egyptians marching after them. So they were very afraid, and the children of Israel cried out to the Lord.

Then they said to Moses:

"Because there were no graves in Egypt, have you taken us away to die in the wilderness? Why have you so dealt with us, to bring us up out of Egypt? Is this not the word that we told you in Egypt, saying, 'Let us alone that we may serve the Egyptians?' For it would have been better for us to serve the Egyptians than that we should die in the wilderness."
(Exodus 14: 11-12)

God was trying to bring the children of Israel into that place of joy, happiness, peace, prosperity and promise-the "Sweet Spot"-yet all the children of Israel could focus on was their problems, fears and issues. God knew that unless He rid them of the "slave" mentality they developed after so many years of serving Egypt, they would never be compelled to seek anything better for themselves. They were dependent upon Pharaoh and Egypt for their well-being yet they feared them greatly. If God had simply brought them out of Egypt and not dealt with Pharaoh, they would never have lived up to the expectations He had for them or fulfill the promise He made to their forefathers. They would always be looking over their shoulders for fear of Pharaoh or his army coming after them. God had to eliminate Pharaoh; otherwise, they would have seen themselves as merely "runaway slaves" on the run from Pharaoh, rather than "free people," freed from Pharaoh by a Mighty God! Their focus would constantly be on their "problem," not their potential, once they left Egypt.

That may be how it is with you right now. You may be so focused on your immediate problem of fear of rejection, failure or lack of money, potential loss of house, car or job, that the very thing that you fear the most has you enslaved mentally, and if you escaped it, doing so would only be temporary. It's just a matter of time before that Giant catches up with you again. Understand this fact, when God delivers you and brings you out of something, it is not temporary, it is permanent:

> *Moses said to the people, "Do not be afraid. Stand still, and see the salvation of the Lord, which He will accomplish for you today. For the Egyptians whom you see today,* **you shall see again no more forever.** *The Lord will fight for you, and you shall hold your peace."*
>
> (Exodus 14: 13-14)

Moses told the people what they needed to hear, but God knew telling them would not be enough. He had to show them in a mighty way that the thing they feared the most would be eliminated from their lives forever, right before their very eyes, and that the God of their forefathers fought for, provided for, cared for and loved them.

He had to bring them to this place and He used Pharaoh to do it. That Giant of a situation, addiction, PAST or person that you fear the most and has you paralyzed will be killed right before your eyes so you will know with certainty it cannot come back to harm you anymore and you can move into the "Sweet Spot" with confidence and assurance. Pharaoh pursued the children of Israel right to where God wanted him to. He positioned the children of Israel right where He wanted them, facing a "sea" of uncertainty, with their backs against a charging Pharaoh and his army:

> And the Lord said to Moses, "Why do you cry to Me, tell the children of Israel to go forward. But lift up your rod, and stretch out your hand over the sea and divide it. And the children of Israel shall go on dry ground through the midst of the sea. And I indeed will harden the hearts of the Egyptians and they shall follow them. So I will gain honor over Pharaoh and over all his army, his chariots, and his horsemen."
> (Exodus 14: 15-17)

God had to get the children of Israel to the point of total dependence and reliance on Him so that they could witness His awesomeness and power as well as see their enemy destroyed, and know that He did it for them. You may be at a "Red Sea" place in your life right now that God has orchestrated to get you to "Go Forward," even though you don't know what "going forward" means right now. In front of you is your Red Sea, behind you is your Giant. You are tempted to turn back from the challenge of changing because you don't see a clear way forward. Going back is not an option even though, like the children of Israel, you think it would be better if you could just go back to what you are used to, not because it is better, but because it is "familiar." So what will you do? Will you go forward and claim your promise and your prize of living in the "Sweet Spot" or will you go backwards and live in regret? I suggest you do what God ordered Moses to tell the children of Israel to do; "Go forward!" March through your "Red Sea," the *sea* of uncertainty, hurt, pain, fear, disappointment, bewilderment, rejection, loss, addiction, whatever your "Red Sea" is, march through it because you know that God is setting your Giant up for its destruction and elimination from your life, and the only way for Him to do it is for YOU to "Go Though it!" Your "Sweet Spot" is on the other side!

Although the issues you face are very real to deal with and the challenge may be great, staying where you are because you are familiar with the situation is hindering you from what God ultimately has for you. The key is to find your way into that place with God where you know that every good thing in your life has already been promised and provided for you, not "someday," but TODAY, just receive it. God hardened Pharaoh and his army's heart to the point where they had to follow the children of Israel into the sea; they had no choice, their days were numbered, so are your Giants:

> ...the Lord caused the sea to go back by a strong east wind all the night, and made the sea into dry land, and the waters were divided. So the children of Israel went into the midst of the sea on the dry ground. And the Egyptians pursued and went after them into the midst of the sea, all Pharaoh's horses, his chariots, and his horsemen. In the morning watch, the Lord looked upon the army of the Egyptians and He troubled the army of the Egyptians. And He took off their chariot wheels, so that they drove them with difficulty; and the Egyptians said, "Let us flee from the face of Israel, for the Lord fights for them against the Egyptians."
>
> (Exodus 14: 21-25)

God opened the sea so that the children of Israel would walk through on "dry ground" and held back the water on both sides as they did. When Pharaoh and his army followed them into the sea, He "troubled" them, meaning He disrupted their ability to gain any ground on the children of Israel; they were set up! Your Giants are being set up, too. Their elimination is crucial to your getting into the "Sweet Spot" with God. Once God got the Egyptians out where He wanted them, He then allowed the waters to cover and drown them so that the children of Israel saw with their own eyes the elimination of their greatest fear and all of his accomplices who could have come back to harm them:

> *Then the Lord said to Moses, "Stretch out your hand over the sea, that the waters may come back upon the Egyptians, on their chariots, and on their horsemen." And Moses stretched out his hand over the sea; and when the morning appeared, the sea returned to its full depth, while the Egyptians were fleeing into it. The waters returned and covered the chariots. The horsemen, and all the army of Pharaoh that came into the sea after them.*
>
> *(Exodus 14: 26-28)*

After God delivered the children of Israel in such a mighty way from the bondage of Pharaoh and Egypt, they found their "Sweet Spot" in their relationship with Him. They saw their enemy destroyed and removed from their lives forever. When David removed Goliath's head from his body, that one act ended any possibility for the giant to come after him "anymore forever." He too enjoyed the "Sweet Spot" with God. To find your "Sweet Spot" with God, talk with Him, fellowship with him, listen for His voice, pray, fast, read and meditate on His word, reflect on your past victories He has brought you through. With any relationship that you want to build, you need to spend some time with that person to get to know them, don't you agree? As you launch your attack, develop the discipline to follow through until you find yourself in the "Sweet Spot" with the knowledge that your Giant was set up to be eliminated from your life.

Here's just a glimpse of some of David's conversations with God during his trials:

> *But his delight is in the law of the Lord, and in His law he meditates day and night. He shall be like a tree planted by the rivers of water, That brings forth its fruit in its season.*
>
> *(Psalm 1: 2-3)*

The steps of a good man are ordered by the Lord, And He delights in his way. Though he fall, he shall not be utterly cast down; For the Lord upholds him with His hand.

(Psalm 37: 23-24)

What is man that You are mindful of him, And the son of man that You visit him?

(Psalm 8: 4)

Along with having fellowship with God, surround yourself with good godly-victory minded people:

Blessed is the man Who walks not in the counsel of the ungodly, Nor stands in the path of sinners, Nor sits in the seat of the scornful:

(Psalm 1: 1)

To continue your journey of discovery, surround yourself with happy, pleasant and peaceful people. Have you noticed how ungodly, negative, bitter, unhappy, sinful and judgmental people weigh you down when you are around them? They seem to have nothing positive to say about anyone or anything? Pessimism is the order of the day for these people, and usually they are the first ones who try to give you counsel? Get away from them; they can only give you what they have! It can be highly contagious. As you find the "Sweet Spot" in your relationship with God, don't let these people drag you into their non-productive, non-profitable world. You have a higher purpose to fulfill and you cannot allow these people to keep you from it. The more you fellowship with God, the more you will want to fellowship with Him. It puts you in a place of AWE and reverence as you enjoy your conversation and interaction with Him on a regular basis.

I delight to do Your will, O my God, And Your law is within my heart. I have proclaimed the good news of righteousness in the great assembly; Indeed, I do not restrain my lips, O Lord, You Yourself know.

(Psalm 40: 8-9)

Great is the Lord, and greatly to be praised.

(Psalm 48: 1)

Cast your burden on the Lord, And He shall sustain you; He shall never permit the righteous to be moved.

(Psalm 55: 22)

Chapter Seven

Be Proactive not Reactive!

O God, You are my God; Early will I seek You; My flesh longs for You in a dry and thirsty land where there is no water. So I have looked for You in the sanctuary, to see Your power and Your glory. Because Your lovingkindness is better than life, My lips shall praise You. Thus I will bless You while I live; I will lift up my hands in Your name. My soul shall be satisfied as the marrow and fatness, And my mouth shall praise You with joyful lips.

(Psalm 63: 1-5)

"There are risks and costs to a program of action. But they are far less that the long-range risks and costs of comfortable inaction."

John F. Kennedy

From the beginning of the encounter between David and Goliath, David was PROACTIVE, and in control of the situation. He called the shots and set the tone for the battle. He didn't wait for the Goliath to seek him out. David sought out Goliath! When David first heard Goliath ranting and raving at the men of Israel, he inquired of one of them asking; "Who is this uncircumcised Philistine that he should defy the armies of the living God?" David wanted to know who is this guy and how dare he defy the armies of my God? David had a problem with Goliath from the start. When Goliath first saw David, I'm sure he didn't give him much thought. He just saw a ruddy looking kid and assumed he wouldn't be a problem; he even called him out to ridicule him, but David didn't react. Instead he said to Goliath, "You come to me with a sword, with a spear, and with a javelin before this day is over, I'll have your head!" Then David attacked Goliath, killed him and took his head from him. David didn't react to Goliath's demands; Goliath reacted to his. This proactive display of faith by David gave the men of Israel an opportunity to gain their courage and to redeem themselves. With Goliath out of the way, they were able to gather the confidence to fight the rest of the Philistine army and defeat them.

You must be the one who's proactively on the attack. Others may be looking to you for courage and leadership as well. Your family or business' survival may be hanging in the balance. You must be the one who calls the shots and sets the tone for the confrontation with your Giants. The reason most people don't prevail is because they are usually reacting to the whims and desires of their Giants. When you are reacting instead of being proactive, you will always be surprised, uncertain and suffer setbacks. Issues will come up at the most inopportune time which causes you to react and do things you wouldn't normally do, like borrow money at unreasonable rates and terms, sell items to get money for drugs, abandon your family, lie, steal and cheat. These kinds of reactions compromise your ability to proactively pursue your Giant with all of your energies and full attention. When you react to the demands of your Giant, you will constantly be thrown off balance and out of sync. In order for you to control the encounter, you must first control your thoughts and actions. If you don't get control of your thoughts and actions, the chances of success for you, your family or business are greatly diminished, and you will find yourself at the mercy of the Giant. When you are not in control, there's always an uneasy feeling that something just isn't right which prevents you from going into the battle with the confidence and assurance of getting the victory.

By being proactive, you, along with God's divine guidance, are the one who plans, decides, and dictates the pace and the outcome of the battle. You choose the time and place and even the weapons of warfare.

One simple and very effective exercise you can use to help you get started towards taking proactive actions to attack your Giants is to ask yourself one question. Come up with at least one response to this question and your answer could help you begin to launch an effective attack.

The question is:

What ONE thing CAN I do, that I am not doing now, that IF I did it, it could make all the difference in my:_____
i.e.: life, home, business, marriage, finances, weight, career, health, relationship, addiction, habit...etc?

Think for a moment, regardless of what it is you're facing, isn't there something you can do to change it if you really wanted to? Nothing is completely out of your control! Complete the sentence for whatever area in your life you want to address, or for each Giant you want to attack. Let this be the first question you ask yourself. Be honest and truthful with your answer. This is the only way this exercise will work for you. You may be tempted to list only the things you will be comfortable doing, but don't just list what you would be comfortable doing. This is why most people are not effective against dealing with their Giants; they only want to do what's comfortable. As I mentioned in an earlier chapter, God is not merely interested in you only doing what's comfortable; He is interested in you doing what you're CAPABLE of doing. Mahatma Gandhi once remarked, "The difference between **what** we do and what we are **capable of doing** would suffice to solve most of the world's problems." God will never give you a desire, without giving you the capability to achieve a result beyond measure.

Waiting to be comfortable causes you to procrastinate, hesitate and deliberate, which in turn causes you to suffer from "paralysis of analysis" where you are so afraid of making a mistake, that you over analyze the solution. You then become paralyzed by inaction and stall until you lose the courage and desire to change. Waiting for everything to be perfect before you take action sets you up for failure from the start. You begin a vicious cycle of procrastination and hesitation, and run the risk of missing your chance to be effective. Timing is critical when attacking your Giants. Bills become late, rent becomes overdue, programs end, deadlines pass, and registrations expire, and so on. Think for a moment. When will conditions ever be perfect enough for you to launch your attack? Never! Stop kidding yourself; you must start now if you want to succeed. Isn't there something you are capable of doing right now that you are not doing that if you did it, it could start to turn the situation you are facing around?

Chances are, what's preventing you from taking the actions necessary for victory is how you *feel* about doing what you CAN versus what you CAN'T! Especially if taking action causes you to be fearful, nervous, anxious, numb or confused. Take for example facing the Giant of looking for a job after a number of years at the same company or months of searching for a job and having little or no success. Unfortunately, with so many layoffs, bankruptcies, and corporate downsizing, many people find themselves facing this Giant. Getting back into the job hunting market after ten or twenty years or more at the same job can be intimidating. The fear of having to go out into the marketplace and fill out job applications, follow up on leads, go through the interviewing process, while at the same time having to market yourself in this new era of "social networking" can be a challenge. It may not be as comfortable as it was in the past, but you can do it. Start with answering the question above, and then set in motion a plan to get it done. Decide what you can do, where you can start, and go from there. Eliminate the urge to let your emotions drive your decisions by focusing on the task at hand. Work tactically. Minimize your fears and maximize your efforts.

As daunting as any task may seem in the beginning, to succeed you have to be proactive and take the actions necessary for success by doing what YOU CAN and trusting God to do the rest. But, don't just stop at one thing. Come up with several actions you can take that you are not taking now, even though it might be uncomfortable at first or that you fear doing. To break the pattern of fear and anxiety you may be experiencing, go for a walk or a jog, workout or exercise. Volunteer at a soup kitchen or a homeless or battered women's shelter. Do something that's considered "out of character" for you. Erase any thoughts of failure from your mind and break those old habit patterns. Stop thinking about it and just do it! Start moving in the direction of your Giants. They will surrender if you proactively get on the offense. Refocus your mind on who you are becoming and where you want to go. Gain the discipline to make the phone calls to potential employers; tell the landlord when you will have the rent or mortgage payment, let the bill collector know when you will have the payment, or that you won't have it by the due date.

I recently had an encounter where I had to be proactive. About three years ago, I co-owned a well known mortgage brokerage firm in Tennessee. The company, as well I, was sued by a disgruntled customer seeking money from any source he could obtain it. He sued everyone associated with the purchase of his home; the real estate agent, real estate company, insurance company, mortgage lender, settlement company, my company and me. It seems he was not happy with the house he purchased and wanted out of the deal. Although I agree with him on some of his argument that his interests were not best served by his realtor and the real estate company he hired to find the property and negotiate the deal for him, but I, nor my company, had anything to do with that part of his transaction. He got a local housing agency involved to bring charges of fraud against all of those who were involved in his purchase of this property and claimed that all of the parties involved conspired to defraud him in this transaction, which is totally impossible. No loan is worth the time and effort it would take to do such a thing. The coordination it would take to pull something like that off just wasn't possible or necessary; besides, there were plenty of good loans to go around. No company would risk their license to operate for one loan.

Anyway, as time went on, he issued his complaint against me and my company, and I became involved in conference after conference, hearing after hearing, constantly spending money and time that I didn't have defending myself from such a frivolous charge. Granted there was and still is fraud going on in the industry, but we weren't involved. Number one because I had no interest, and number two, it wasn't worth it. There was always plenty of good business in the marketplace, and we chose to go after that business. There is never a need to conspire against any borrower and defraud them. After four years of back and forth with this case, and having his attorneys try to force the other parties to settle and pay this man some money, to no avail, they finally got around to dealing solely with me and his charge against me. Of course he had his attorneys from the area legal services agency (Goliath), and I had already spent a lot of money on my attorneys over the months leading up to this time, so I had had enough. I was not going to continue this costly back and forth charade and decided to be PROACTIVE and take the case to trial. I was not going to settle with him. I was not going to pay him a dime that I didn't owe him, and they were not going to intimidate me into doing so. When it came time for the last pretrial deposition hearing before setting a trial date, I informed the judge that I was dismissing my attorney and would be representing myself at the trial. Maybe he thought that was a dumb move and tried to discourage me from doing so, but I decided to take my chances with God and The Holy Spirit as my representation! At the deposition, there I was sitting across the conference room table with THREE of their attorneys, the court stenographer, and THE PLAINTIFF on his side, and God, the Holy Spirit and me on my side answering questions and firing back at them with no hesitation or fear!

God and the Holy Spirit represented me; I was just the vessel He used to show His power and protection. He gave me the confidence to proactively attack my accuser and his attorneys, and a peace of mind to do it that is indescribable! When you proactively attack your Giant with God's help, it transcends anything you have ever experienced. God knew I had nothing to hide, and He defended me to the fullest. About a month later I got a call from the court, the plaintiff's attorneys wanted to have another arbitration hearing to seek a settlement, and I told them no, I wanted to take this to trial and that there was nothing for me to arbitrate about. We set a follow up date a week later where all parties would discuss the setting of a trial date. On the date of the follow up session, the judge's office called me to inform me that the plaintiff's attorney wanted to make an announcement. When he got on the phone, he informed me that they were putting forth a motion to "Dismiss the case" against me, and that they would be dropping the charges with the court as of that day! Hallelujah! God is truly able to fight for you if you PROACTIVELY attack and not react to the whims of the Giant! I did and I won! So will you!

You are always capable of doing something to confront your Giants, regardless of what they may be. Don't give in to the impulse to quit or avoid confronting the issues. Feel the fear, hurt, anxiety, numbness and confusion and attack anyway! You will find that once you do, what you've feared or felt anxious about is never as bad as you told yourself it would be and it gets easier each time you do it. Can you pray and seek God's guidance, protection and direction in this situation? That's being capable and proactive. You can forgive, refocus your attention, gather stones, make the phone call, seek medical attention, seek spiritual guidance, attend church, swallow your pride, ask forgiveness, stop gossiping, be honest, be truthful, open your heart, open your mind, go back to school, look for a better job, move away from your abuser, or call the mortgage, auto or credit company.... etc., can't you? These are all examples of being proactive. As you can see, there are several actions you can proactively take to move towards confronting your Giants. You are never helpless or hopeless.

Slay one Giant and others will follow

Also, as I studied this account of David, Goliath and the Philistines, there was another thing that stood out to me about the story that I hadn't noticed before or heard anyone mention much about. Here's what I discovered:

> *So the Philistine came, and began drawing near to David, and*
> *THE MAN WHO BORE THE SHIELD WENT BEFORE HIM.*
> *(1 Samuel 17: 41)*

Did you notice it? Goliath wasn't alone; he had a shield bearer, a man who carried his shield for him when he went into battle. This man went out in front of Goliath, so we know he was around the action. But, what happened to him? Where did he go? We don't hear about him being engaged in the fight. In fact, we don't hear anything else about him. I think I know why! In the past, when men had to face Goliath, the shield bearer noticed that most of them ran away as fast as they could before the battle began, but on this day, he saw that David was not running away from him. Instead David ran TOWARDS Goliath with a confidence and determinations to overcome the giant unlike any man he had seen do before him. Thus, I believe the shield bearer feared David and FLED the scene! It will seem that way when you are at the point of confrontation with your Giants, also.

At first it will seem as if there are other people, situations or circumstances surrounding your Giants making them *appear* to be larger than they really are and harder to defeat than you originally thought. It will appear that there's more trouble, strife or accomplices to deal with; whatever the case, they just don't seem to be alone. The FEAR (False Evidence Appearing Real) of having to fight these other Giants increases as they all seem to be aligned against you. Not only did Goliath have a shield bearer to accompany him into battle, but he also had over six thousand fighting men of the Philistine army. You will find that as you get into the battle, the opposite is true. Once you conquer and defeat one Giant, many of the others you've feared seem to disappear like Goliath's shield bearer. These can be co-workers, family members, church members, illnesses, a drug addiction or your current financial situation; whatever, their ability to threaten you is gone when their leader's power is removed!

Think back to when you were in grade school and there was a bully on the playground who always picked on you or the other kids. Didn't there seem to be other kids who followed the bully everywhere they went? They were called "sidekicks." Did you ever notice that when you or one of the other kids decided that you were going to stand up to this bully and not be bullied any longer, that you were going to fight back, win or lose, you were not going to take it anymore, this is when the sidekicks would flee from around the bully and leave them to fight for themselves like Goliath's shield bearer? When this happens, the bully does what Goliath did next. He started getting loud and boisterous and tried to use his old intimidation tactics to scare David off, because he really didn't want to fight him, and neither does your Giant want to fight you:

> *And the Philistine looked about and saw David; he disdained him; for he was only a youth, ruddy and good-looking. So the Philistine said to David, "Am I a dog that you come to me with sticks?" And the Philistine cursed David by his gods. And the Philistine said to David, come to me, and I will give your flesh to the birds of the air and the vests of the field!"*
> *(1 Samuel 17: 42-44)*

Now Goliath is daring David to come to him. That doesn't sound like someone who is being the aggressor in a fight to me, what about you? That's how it is with your Giant when it appears they will have to fight you. They will get louder and more boisterous, trying to intimidate you and scare you off, because they really aren't too eager to engage you in battle. Face your Giants and the others will flee or at least their power and influence over you will be diminished. Also, as you proactively attack your Giants, you will find yourself gaining the confidence and experience that will enable you to live victoriously in the face of seemingly insurmountable odds and challenges.

Chapter Eight

The Natural vs. The Spiritual

Finally, my brethren, be strong in the Lord and in the power of HIS might. Put on the whole armor of God that you may be able to stand against the wiles of the devil. For we do not wrestle against flesh and blood, but against principalities, against powers, against the rulers of the darkness of this age, against SPIRITUAL hosts of wickedness in the heavenly places.
(Ephesians 6: 10-12)

"Man often becomes what he believes Himself to be...If I have the belief that I can do it, I shall surely acquire the capacity to do it even if I may not have it in the beginning."

Mahatma Gandhi

Living in the "*natural*" means you are operating in the *flesh*. In the natural, David did not match up to Goliath in any way. Goliath's size was superior, his strength was superior, his armor was superior, his sword was superior, his army was superior, his battle experience and reputation were superior, all of the tangible things we tend to look at on the surface looked superior; however, none of that mattered to David. It may have mattered to Goliath and his Philistine army; it may have mattered to the men of Israel who feared Goliath; it may have even mattered to the people in the land who came to see the fight; all of these things may have mattered to everyone except David. David knew how to keep the main thing the main thing, and he knew that what he had going for him had been the only thing that mattered in a spiritual battle. Even though the natural things of Goliath were superior to those of David's, the ONE and ONLY thing that mattered to David was the fact that he knew:

HIS GOD WAS SUPERIOR!

> *Then David said to the Philistine, "You come to me with a sword, with a spear, and with a javelin. But I come to you IN THE NAME OF THE LORD OF HOSTS, THE GOD of the armies of Israel."*
>
> *(1 Samuel 17: 45)*

God was not only his equalizer, but He gave David the overwhelming advantage! The two didn't compare. Goliath's armor and experience didn't matter. When it comes to spiritual warfare, the natural things of man will NEVER defeat the spiritual things of God. The war with your Giants is not fought in the natural realm, but the spiritual, and must be spiritually discerned. The Apostle Paul, while addressing the people of Corinth, admonished them to consider a vital fact in dealing with the spiritual and the natural:

> *. . . My speech and my preaching were not with persuasive words of human wisdom, but in demonstration of the Spirit and of power, that your faith should not be in the wisdom of men but in the power of God. But God has revealed them to us through His Spirit. For what man knows the things of a man except the spirit of the man which is in him? No one knows the things of God except the Spirit of God. Now we have not received the spirit of the world, but the Spirit who is from God, that we might know THE THINGS that have been freely given to us by God. These things we also speak, not in words which man's wisdom teaches but which the Holy Spirit teaches, comparing spiritual things with spiritual. But the natural man does not receive the things of the Spirit of God, for they are foolishness to him; nor can he know them, because they are spiritually discerned.*
>
> *(1 Corinthians 2: 4-5, 10-14)*

The Natural

Things that are "*NATURAL*" are thoughts that come from your *HEAD* and are manifested in the physical realm. You are operating in the natural when you rely on tangible things that you can see, touch, and smell, hear or taste using your physical senses, reasoning ability or willpower. When you depend on your physical abilities or someone else's to solve your problems, you limit your ability to discern the things that are spiritual. Your education, money, good looks, house, upbringing and pedigree has no effect against spiritual devices. Many times when things that are spiritual manifest in the natural, they cause you to suffer a loss or setback of some kind. Maybe you are about to lose your home to foreclosure, your automobile is about to be repossessed, or you are about to lose your job and your debts are piling up. These Giants pose a real threat, and therefore they have a paralyzing effect on you. Perhaps you may have to confront a loved one or a beloved entity such as your church, job, organization, social or civic organization, which could result in hurt feelings, loss of relationship, separation, divorce, severed friendships and family ties. Real or imagined, they can cause turmoil and confusion in your life.

Spiritual Giants manifesting through natural means can disrupt your peace of mind, well being and security. While it may be painful and embarrassing to have to go through it in the natural, spiritually this could be the freeing experience you needed to prepare you to achieve the higher purpose God has for your life. Although you may feel you've failed if you lost your marriage, home, job, church, automobile, or you've had to file a personal or business bankruptcy, it wouldn't be the end of your ability to get any of it again. You can recover. Remember, in the natural, David had it all it seemed; two wives, children, home, everything, yet when he took his eyes off of the source of all his blessings and followed his fears instead of his faith and joined the Philistines, he lost it all. Satan (the demonic spirit) had influence in David's life and it is suspected that he was present during every trial David went through. However, when David got his spirit back in alignment with God's purpose for his life, he recovered it all again. He went to God and asked Him to lead him towards regaining his family and possessions. So can you. Not only did God restore David's family and possessions, but He also gave him back much more than he had lost. More importantly, during this process, David examined his spiritual relationship with God and found it was lacking. He then committed himself to restoring their relationship.

The same happened with Job, a wealthy man in the Bible in whom God found favor. Job lost it all when Satan (the demonic spirit) asked God if he could afflict Job with trouble and strife as a test of God and Job's relationship. God consented. In the natural, Job seemed to have it all, too; a loving wife, houses, land, children, friends, livestock, but in the final analysis, he found his spiritual relationship with God was subordinate to the natural things in his life. Even though Job did not sin or curse God during the process of discovering his lack, it still revealed deficiencies in his relationship with God. After the test with Satan, God restored Job two fold giving him "double for his trouble."

The common denominator in both of these encounters is the presence and influence of Satan. Tests and trials are inevitable; you are going to have them, but God gives you the ability to deal with them when they do. Demonic spirits will always attack you in the natural-your marriage, home, family, career, business- to try to get you to give up and quit. As He did with David and Job, God sometimes allow these attacks to happen to you. Don't get discouraged when they do, for He allows them for a reason. Usually the reason is for you to discover the deficiencies in your relationship with Him and He gives you the opportunity to address it, correct it and live free from fear, lack and strife.

If you are wondering why you haven't been successful in defeating the Giants in your life, maybe it's because you are trying to fight a spiritual Giant with limited natural and carnal means and understanding. If they are superior to you physically, in their armor, in their armies, in their financial and educational resources, as well as in their emotional fortitude and mental superiority (real or imagined), then you will continue to be defeated every time you have an encounter with them. Your efforts to prevail against them will be futile at best. These Giants must be attacked, conquered and defeated with spiritual warfare. Giants of drug, alcohol and substance addiction, sexual perversion, homosexuality, promiscuity, physical and mental abuse and pornography are spiritual demons that try to destroy your very existence. They can be conquered if they are addressed with the proper "spiritual" weapons of warfare.

The Spiritual

> *"...For the Lord does not see as man sees; from man looks at the outward appearance, but the Lord looks at the heart."*
> *(1 Samuel 16: 7)*

On the other hand, the things that are *SPIRITUAL* are desires that come from the *HEART!* God looks at your heart. This is where He resides. The scripture says 'the natural or carnal man cannot discern the things that are of the spirit.' The *spiritual* realm is the intangible; you can't see it, smell it, touch it, hear or taste it. You access things of the spirit through *faith* in your heart for the things of God; therefore, spiritual Giants require a different mindset and understanding. They must be spiritually discerned. As I pointed out earlier, you will not defeat a spiritual Giant with natural or carnal means. This will take a more aggressive approach. Spiritual Giants seek to destroy you, not just hinder your progress. You have to totally submit to the will of God and get into an attitude of prayer, supplication, consecration, and repentance to conquer them.

If you want to attack your spiritual Giants with lasting success, start by resetting your focus and reassessing the nature of your attack. You need to have a "Heart Attack" yes a "Heart Attack.!" I'm not talking about the medical kind (smile); I'm talking about the spiritual kind. In the past, you have been attacking your spiritual Giants using a "Head Attack," which explains why your efforts have been limited. When you attack your Giants with your head, you are using your thinking, willpower, reasoning abilities and knowledge to prevail. However, these are limited because your success is often determined by your emotions, how you FEEL, but feelings can be misleading! When you attack with your "heart" your attack is with passion, commitment, determination and persistence; you are relentless in your efforts to see the results you desire! By attacking your Giants with your heart, you are utilizing God's power and promise of deliverance, favor, help and hope, coupled with your faith, belief, trust and a spiritual discernment to succeed. Discern what's in your heart. God is the only one able to help you boldly attack and defeat your Giants with lasting success. Your heart is the key to receiving everything from Him. King Solomon, David's son, discovered how important what's in one's heart is to God:

> *At Gibeon the Lord appeared to Solomon in a dream by night; and God said," Ask! What shall I give you?" And Solomon said: "You have shown great mercy to Your servant David my father, because he walked before You in truth, in righteousness, and in uprightness of heart with You; You have continued this great kindness for him,.... Now, O Lord my God, You have made Your servant king instead of my father David, but I am a little child; I do not know how to go out or come in., And Your servant is in the midst of Your people who You have chosen, a great people, too numerous to be numbered or counted. Therefore give to Your servant an understanding HEART to judge Your people,... The speech pleased the Lord. Then God said to him: "Because you have asked this thing, and have not asked long life for yourself, nor have you asked riches for yourself, nor have you asked for the life of your enemies, but you asked for yourself to discern justice, behold I have done ACCORDING TO YOUR WORDS; see I have given you a wise and understanding HEART,... AND I have also given you what you have not asked: BOTH riches and honor,"*
>
> *(1 Kings 3: 5-6, 7: 10-13)*

The heart is where God grants you your desires according to His will and purpose. Whatever is in your heart, good or bad, will manifest sooner or later in the deeds and the actions you take. Although David and his son Solomon both had their issues and erred during their reigns, they both were good hearted kings; therefore, God continued to bless and show favor towards them:

> Now it was in the HEART of David to build a temple for the name of the Lord God of Israel, But the Lord said to my father David, "Whereas it was in your HEART to build a temple for My name, you did well in that IT WAS IN YOUR HEART. Nevertheless you shall not build the temple, but your son who will come from your body; he shall build the temple for My name."
>
> (2 Chronicles 6: 7-9)

You don't have to be perfect to receive help with your Giants from God; He already knows what's in your heart, but you should examine it for purity and truth when you ask God to help you in your attack. Examine your motives. He saw that David had it in his heart to build a temple for Him, and even though God chose David's son Solomon to build His temple, He was pleased with the desire David had in his heart and that was enough. David had his issues just like all of us, yet God saw that he was a sincere man with honor, integrity and reverence for the things of God. David was able to not only defeat Goliath, a physical giant, but he was able to defeat many of the spiritual Giants that came into his life physically, emotionally and mentally through constant prayer, fellowship with God and sincere repentance. David called upon God to help him through his most difficult times and to change him from the "inside" out where it counts:

> Create in me a clean heart, O God, and RENEW a steadfast SPIRIT within me. Do not cast me away from Your presence, And do not take YOUR Holy Spirit from me.
>
> (Psalm 51: 10-11)

God blessed and kept David through all of his mishaps, missteps, and the ups and downs of being human, through his triumphs and tragedies, through his joys and jolts, his pleasure and pain. He overlooked many of David's faults because his heart remained true to Him always.

God (The Creator) communicates with man (His creation) through a *heart of faith.* You may be having trouble breaking free of addictions and other spiritual Giants because you are trying to fight a *spiritual* Giant with your head in the natural and not with your *heart,* the spirit. This kind of approach will be a constant struggle because you are trying to use willpower, positive thinking, or some other self-prescribed method. None of which spiritual Giants respond to and if they did, the results would only be temporary. Sooner or later you will find yourself dealing with the same old struggle again and again. It's like people who stop doing drugs or stop smoking for a while, just to have the habit resurface later. Your willpower will only last so long. These demons will, however, respond permanently to the Word of God:

> *For the word of God is living and powerful, and sharper than any two-edged sword, piercing even to the division of soul and spirit, and of joints and marrow, and is a discerner of the thought and intents of the heart.*
>
> *(Hebrews 4:12)*

The most significant evidence you will have as proof that you have conquered a Giant in your life is when you have a "CHANGE OF HEART" about what you are facing. When you have a change of heart about a situation, person, event, drug, vice, sexual perversion, or any spiritual Giant hindering your life, God has released you from the stronghold and grip the addiction or fear had on you. When you have a change of heart towards something or someone, there is a difference in your attitude, outlook, and pursuits. As God takes the desire you had for those destructive vices, habits and people away, you will no longer have the constant mental and emotional, back and forth battles you've had in the past when you tried to use willpower or positive thinking to deal with your Giants. Nor will you have to wrestle with trying not to think about doing the things you've done in the past because you will no longer have the desire for that type of behavior or those destructive vices.

Think of something or someone you've had a change of heart about in your life; perhaps a relationship, drug habit, financial situation, emotional PAST, etc. How do you feel about it or them now? What effect does it have on you? How much thought do you give it or them? Not much, I imagine. If you really want to attack this Giant and be delivered from it like in the past, go to God in earnest and sincere prayer with repentance and ask Him to deliver you from it. Ask Him to take away your desire and lust for it; ask in faith and from your heart. The following prayers are from David when he was battling his Giants in the flesh:

> *Hear my prayer, O Lord, and let my cry come to You. Do not hide Your face from me in the day of my trouble; Incline Your ear to me; In the day that I call, answer me speedily. For my days are consumed like smoke, and my bones are burned like a hearth. My heart is stricken and withered like grass, So that I forget to eat my bread, Because of the sound of my groaning, my bones cling to my skin. My enemies reproach me all day long; Those who deride me swear an oath against me, But You O Lord, shall endure forever, and the remembrance of Your name to all generations.*
> *(Psalm 102: 1-5, 8, 12)*

> *Bless the Lord, O my soul; And all that is within me, bless His holy name! Bless the Lord, O my soul, And forget not all your benefits: Who forgives all your iniquities, Who heals all your diseases, Who redeems your life from destruction, Who crowns you with loving-kindness and tender mercies, Who satisfies your mouth with good things, So that your youth is renewed like the eagle's. The Lord is merciful and gracious, Slow to anger, and abounding in mercy.*
> *(Psalm 103: 1-5, 8)*

As you earnestly seek God's divine protection and help, He will answer you by giving you the ability to courageously attack and conquer your Giants from the inside out. It may not be an instant victory, but then again it might; I've seen it happen. I advise you to keep seeking God's grace, mercy, and support even when you don't see an immediate change. Stay encouraged and focused, for in due season you will get your breakthrough and the victory. When you were preoccupied with your Giants, they consumed you, your time, your family, your mind, your money and your resources. You lusted after it often at the expense and sacrifice of others. Now that you have killed it in your heart, that's doesn't mean the consequences of your actions will disappear overnight either. There may be some healing that needs to take place. Don't expect everything to necessarily go back to the way it was before this happened. Everybody won't be happy for you. Trust has been violated, money was stolen, countless promises were made and broken, excuses were offered and outright lies were told. Although the drugs, sex, alcohol, food, anger or fear that once had you hooked, bound and tied up mentally in financial straits or emotional turmoil no longer have a hold of you, changing other people's perception of you can take a while! There are some things that only time can heal.

The Difference

How do you know when you are operating in the natural versus the spiritual? Many times other people bring issues into your life. Learn to discern these destructive people and their vices. You can usually tell when you are communicating with someone who is operating in the natural; it will seem as if they are working an agenda in their effort to impose their views, values and vices on you and your life. Be cautious in how you relate to them. These workers of iniquity will try to appeal to your logic and reasoning and try to make you feel guilty or obligated about something you did or didn't do for them. Be leery of these people and their spirit; it's contagious. On the other hand, if someone is appealing to you in the spirit, their appeal would usually be an emotional-heart-to-heart connection. You feel their sincerity and honesty. There's no pressure for you to think like they think or do as they do. Jesus spoke to man's heart, not his head.

First, begin by recognizing that God is a *'Spirit.'* Since He is a Spirit this is how you are to worship Him:

> *"The hour is coming, and now is, when the true worshipers will worship the Father in spirit and in truth; for the Father is seeking such to worship Him.* **GOD IS SPIRIT** *and those who worship Him MUST worship Him in SPIRIT and in TRUTH."*
>
> *(John 4: 23-24)*

I know people both personally and professionally, as well as major stars and entertainers, who have had to experience battling spiritual Giants of drug, alcohol and sex addictions, as well as suffered tremendous financial loss. Although I've never had to deal with any addictions, I've have experienced great financial loss, and believe me, as painful as it may be going through the process, you will get over it! It may be uncomfortable at the time, but if you keep it in perspective, pray for guidance and strength and be persistent, you can overcome this. Sometimes you have to GIVE IT UP to GO UP! These Giants mentally, physically and emotionally weigh you down and they tempt you to sin in ways you never would have thought of had you not been trying to hold on to them. Old habits, emotions, attitudes, hurts, losses, relationships, mindsets and thinking threatens to keep you in spiritual bondage and tied to unhealthy relationships and situations. This in turn causes you to repeat the bad behavior patterns that led to you being where you are in the first place. God is stripping you from that bondage. Spiritual Giants keep you bound because of habit and fear of change, and you may be trying to hold on to these past destructive behaviors even though they no longer serve any productive or profitable use in your life. You must let go of them. God will forgive ignorance, but He despises *disobedience.* When you learn better you should do better. The process may be painful, but it is necessary to rid you of this Giant. Know that God's plan is one hundred times better than anything you can rig up on our own. As you begin to operate in the spirit, you will find yourself trusting God for the answers, solutions and outcomes to the issues in your life that you once tried to handle yourself. You stop worrying and start praying about resolutions. Giants you were once too afraid to confront, you stop hiding from.

This may also be a test of your faith. Although God doesn't play games with His children, He does chastise you when you go astray, like any loving Father would. Some of the drug and alcohol use, financial decisions, unhealthy personal and professional relationships and career choices that you made, chances are you knew that they could lead to trouble, but you proceeded to do it anyway. Remember, you decided to buy the drugs, liquor, house, car, boat, start dating and even marry the person anyway, knowing it wasn't the best thing for you, but you thought you could handle it.

God might be trying to free you from the bondage of these situations or people, and take you higher and make you stronger in your faith:

Let us lay aside every weight, and the sin which so easily ensnares us, and let us run with ENDURANCE the race that is before us, looking unto Jesus, the author and finisher of our faith who for the joy that was set before Him ENDURED the cross, despising the shame, and has sat down at the right hand of the throne of God.

(Hebrews 12: 1-2)

	Natural/Carnal		Spiritual
God:	Rely on your head	vs.	Rely on your heart
Marriage:	Convenience, status	vs.	Committed, united
Money:	Lack, inconsistent	vs.	Perpetual, abundant
Relationships:	Temporary, selfish	vs.	Lasting, genuine, enduring
Love:	Conditional, non-committal	vs.	Unconditional, committed
Warfare:	By sight, self reliance,	vs.	Faith, rely on God

There's a distinct difference between the two. Have you been natural or spiritually minded in your outlook? If it is the former, you may have to "Go Through, to get to," in terms of changing your perspective. It may be shameful, embarrassing, humiliating and uncomfortable, but necessary to bring you to where you need to be in life and in your relationship with God. Overcoming a challenge is sometimes necessary so that you can see God move in your life.

Think about the follow statement for a moment:

You can't have a Victory without a Fight!

How would you know you've won a victory if you've never had to fight in the first place? Don't run from the fight, it has a purpose. If God led you to it, you must go through it. He could be correcting something in your character. He knows you are better than you've displayed in the past and sometimes He has to get your attention to bring you around to realizing for yourself:

> *"My son, do not despise the chastening of the Lord, nor be discouraged when you are rebuked by Him; For whom the Lord loves He chastens, And scourges every son whom He receives." Now no chastening seems to be joyful for the present, but painful; nevertheless, afterwards it yields the peaceable fruit of righteousness to those who have been trained by it.*
> *(Hebrews 12: 5-6, 11)*

There you have it. This accounting of how David attacked and defeated his giant Goliath, as well as how he addressed other areas of his life that you can relate to, attest to the fact that you don't have to be perfect to have favor with God and conquer your Giants either. Attacking the Giants in your life may not be easy, but congratulations on your decision to go after those things which threaten your joy, peace, happiness and purpose God has for you and your family. Like you, David seemed to be at a disadvantage when he faced the giant Goliath, but David had the **ONE** thing going for him that mattered most, *David had God on his side*, and so do you. That makes all the difference in any fight. If your peace of mind, security, and the well being of your family, business, career or organization is hanging in the balance, it's time to implement your plan of attack! By applying the principles and developing the mindset of David, "A man after God's own heart" and a giant killer, you, too, can attack and defeat your Giants regardless of what your circumstances may be or how big they are.

David faced Goliath with no fear. He had the assurance that God would help him defeat Goliath, and so should you. Today is the day, now is the time, this is the place for you to make your stand. No more running, hiding, or living in fear or doubt. You will be victorious and prevail over your Giants. Get ready, reset your focus, strengthen your resolve, and seek God's direction and protection for victory. You have the transforming favor of God's grace upon your life. See you in the victor's circle!

ATTACK YOUR GIANTS!
God Has Blessed!

Giant Slayers Declaration

I, _____, hereby declare as of this day: _____ by the power of Almighty God and the love of my Lord and Savior Jesus Christ, through the help, nurturing, guidance and power of the Holy Ghost that I will defeat the Giant of_____ that I face.

_____ you have no more power over me or my _____ any longer. I declare and decree you null and void in my life. I make this declaration, as I stand on the promise God made to the children of Israel of which I am an heir in which He declares:

> *"No weapon that is formed against thee shall prosper; and every tongue that shall rise against thee in judgment thou shalt condemn. This is the heritage of the servants of the Lord, and their righteousness is of me," saith the Lord.*
>
> *(Isaiah 54: 17 KJV)*

I believe it and receive it in the name of Jesus Christ. All of my debts are paid, your tricks and schemes are cancelled, and I have the victory as promised to me by the Lord My God in the name of my Lord and Savior, Jesus Christ. It is done according to my faith.

About the Author

Donnye D. Collins, Sr. is the Founder and President of Collins Spiritual Construction Ministries. He is an avid student of the Bible, a writer and publisher of Christian leadership based publications. Donnye is also a highly sought after dynamic speaker, teacher, and master at inspiring people in both the Christian and corporate environment. As a former co-owner of two mortgage brokerage and real estate investment firms as well as an entrepreneur and business owner owning multiple businesses through the years, Donnye understands the dynamics of "slaying Giants!"

He is the proud father of daughter, Tranise and son, Donnye, Jr. as well as an exceptionally proud grandfather of Terryen and Asia, and resides with his wonderful wife Christine in Maryland.

Also, get the companion; *Attack Your Giants Workbook, Journal, CD* and other merchandise at www.attackyour giants.com.

Like David's, your story of victory and triumph can be a tremendous blessing and inspiration to someone and I invite you to share it. Join my *"Giant Slayers"* blog at: *http://attackyourgiants.blogspot.com/* and share with us how you "attacked your Giants" and **WON!**

Connect with Donnye on Facebook, MySpace, and Twitter for future events and happenings coming soon to your area.

Other publications coming soon from Donnye D. Collins, Sr.:

Your PAIN Was Planned! *Using Joseph's Perspective to Overcome any Setback, Setup or Situation and Succeed!* and KEEP YOUR FORK...THE BEST IS YET TO COME!

Feel the *POWER* of a live transformational encounter with the author. To book Donnye for your upcoming workshop, conference, seminar or meeting please contact CSCM Management, LLC at 410-200-0111, or write and inquire to:

CSCM Management, LLC
13017 Wisteria Dr.
Suite 123
Germantown, MD 20874

Make a Difference

*Then they brought the little children to Him, that He might touch them, but the disciples rebuked those who brought them. But when Jesus saw it, He was greatly displeased and said to them, "Let the little children come to Me, and do not forbid them; for of such is the kingdom of God." And He took them up in His arms, laid **His** hands on them, and blessed them.*

(Mark 10: 13-16)

Donnye truly believes in giving, especially to causes that benefit children. Therefore, because of the incredible work they do every day, he has made arrangements for part of the proceeds from the sale of this book to be donated to the charities and causes that are dear to him and his family. Listed are those charities:

The Children's Hunger Fund: www.chfus.org
Feed The Children: www.feedthechildren.org
St. Jude Children's Research Hospital: www.stjude.org
Children's Health Fund: www.childrenshealthfund.org
The Children Aid Society: www.childrensaidsociety.org

For more information on how you can help, please log on to the websites provided, or contact Donnye at donnye@spiritualconstruction.com.